THE GILDS OF CHINA

WITH AN ACCOUNT OF
THE GILD MERCHANT
OR CO-HONG OF CANTON

BY

HOSEA BALLOU MORSE, LL.D.
SOMETIME STATISTICAL SECRETARY, INSPECTORATE
GENERAL OF CUSTOMS, CHINA

SECOND EDITION

NEW YORK / RUSSELL & RUSSELL

FIRST PUBLISHED IN 1932
REISSUED, 1967, BY RUSSELL & RUSSELL
A DIVISION OF ATHENEUM HOUSE, INC.
BY ARRANGEMENT WITH THE ESTATE OF H. B. MORSE
L. C. CATALOG CARD NO.: 66–24733

THE GILDS OF CHINA

PREFACE

In first approaching the subject treated in this booklet, my intention was to write a review article which should compare and contrast the organisation and working of gilds in China and in the Western world. My writing soon over-ran the space which any review editor could grant to such a subject; and I found, moreover, that the information at my disposal on Chinese gilds was mainly in the shape of *matériel pour servir*, and that, properly speaking, no analysed account of the gild system was available. I was accordingly led further into my subject than had been my original intention. I might even have gone further and, by diluting freely, have made more of a book; but I trust that those who may read this compact booklet will find that the information contained in it will satisfy their requirements.

I bring to the subject a certain degree of personal knowledge, but I have always referred to information already in print, whenever it existed. Where there is no reference to other authorities, the fact stated must be accepted on my own authority, either from my personal observation, or coming from my study of Chinese history and social institutions.

Among the authorities cited, none has greater weight on Chinese gilds than Dr. Daniel J. Macgowan. An American citizen of the best type and duly qualified Doctor in Medicine, he entered on medical mission work at an early age; and he threw himself so heartily into the work that, in 1855, he refused the post of American Consular Agent at Ningpo, on the ground that he " had no time for other occupations." He found time, however, to contribute to the Journal of the North-China Branch of the Royal Asiatic Society on its first organisation in 1857; and he wrote frequently, and on many subjects, for nearly forty years, up nearly to his death, an octogenarian passed; his valuable monograph on Chinese gilds in 1889 being one of his latest. It is an honour to follow in the steps of this cheery and hard-working sinologue.

H. B. M.

EWELL, *May* 1909.

CONTENTS

	PAGE
INTRODUCTORY	1
Political conditions affecting Chinese and European gilds	1
Economic conditions affecting Chinese and European gilds	2
Accumulation of capital in China and Europe . .	4
Protection given by the law in China and Europe .	5
THE RELIGIOUS FRATERNITY	7
THE CRAFT GILD	11
Origin of Gilds: in England	13
in China	13
Membership: in England	14
in China	14
Government: in England	15
in China	16
Income: in England	17
in China	17
Common Worship: in England	20
in China	21
Control of Trade:	
in England	22
in China	24
Silk Gild at Shanghai	25
Bankers' Gild at Shanghai	25
Bankers' Gild at Ningpo	26
Bankers' Gild at Wuhu	26
Tea Gild at Shanghai	26
Opium Gild at Wuchow	27
Druggists' Gild at Wenchow	27
Fishmongers' Gild at Ningpo	27
Millers' Gild at Wenchow	28
Standard Measures	28
Jurisdiction over Members:	
in England	29
in China	31
Tea Gild at Hankow	32
Opium Gild at Ningpo	33

PAGE

Jurisdiction over Members in China (*Contd.*).—
    Silkweavers' Gild at Wenchow . . . 33
    Goldbeaters' Gild at Soochow 33
    Wheelbarrow Gild at Shanghai . . . 34
    Servants' Gild at Shanghai 35
    Journeymen : in England 35
           in China 36
    Apprentices : in England 36
           in China . . . . . . , 37
THE PROVINCIAL CLUB 39
    Origin 42
    Membership 42
    Government 43
    Income 44
    Common worship 45
    Control of Trade 46
    Hanyang Club at Ichang 47
    Shantung Club at Ningpo 48
    Jurisdiction over Members 49
    Disputes between members and non-members . 50
    Protection against officials 51
    " Ningpo Joss-house " riots at Shanghai, 1874 and
        1898 52
THE GILD MERCHANT 55
    The Gild of Newchwang 57
    Purposes and income 57
    Regulations for the assay of silver . . . 58
    Rules for exchange transactions . . . 59
    Rules for regulating the grain market . . 59
    Use of transfer money instead of cash . . 60
    The Swatow Gild 61
    Government, democratic in form . . . 61
    Income 62
    Purposes 63
    Methods of procedure in disputes . . . 63
    The Canton Co-hong and Factories . . . 65
    Canton the staple for foreign trade . . 65
    Beginnings of foreign trade with China . . 66
    The gild merchant in England . . . 67
    Character of English foreign trade . . . 69
    Restrictions on aliens in England . . . 69
    Restrictions alternately relaxed and re-imposed 70
    Correspondence between Chinese and English gilds 72
    Growth of restrictions on aliens at Canton . 73
    First formation of Co-hong in 1720 . . . 74

CONTENTS

PAGE

Final organisation of Co-hong in 1782 . . . 77
The office of Hoppo at Canton 79
The Vicerory and other provincial officials . . 79
Regulations restricting the liberty of foreigners . 80
Effect on traders' business 83
Regulation of foreign shipping 84
Selling of imports and buying of exports . . 85
Co-hong supported by Chinese officials . . . 87
Results of working of Co-hong 88
Foreign trade chiefly English and American . . 90
The Canton gild merchant abolished . . . 92
APPENDIX : Rules of Gilda Carpentar, London . . . 95
WORKS CITED 101
INDEX 105

THE GILDS OF CHINA

THE GILDS OF CHINA

INTRODUCTORY

In her gilds, as in so many others of her institutions, China illustrates for us Europe as it was in the Middle Ages; but, while the points of resemblance are numerous, there are many differences, all equally illuminative of the differences between the social and political organisation of the East and of the West. In China we have had for centuries a theoretically autocratic government, working through a bureaucracy which, though appointed by the autocracy, has been and is in many respects independent of it, and, though drawn from the people, is no longer in touch with them; while the people, so long as the taxes were duly paid and while there was no serious disturbance, have lived their own life of trader and farmer, in democratic equality and, for all essentials of life, in freedom, asking only that the bureaucracy should leave them alone, and organising politically only for two purposes—protection or protest against the acts of commission and of omission by their officials, and rebellion. In Europe we have had, during the period of greatest gild activity, sovereigns playing their people against the pretensions of the feudal nobility, and a nobility which aimed at the absorption of all executive office and was often driven to ally itself with the burgesses against the centralising policy of the king; while the people, conscious of their own claims, were often provided, now by the king, now by the support of their feudal lords, with weapons by which they were enabled to secure a step ahead toward the municipal authority they ultimately reached.   In England, to take that alone of the countries of Europe, we have seen the common law developed under the impulse of the people and becoming the paramount law of the realm, to which the king's ministers and servants and the king's subjects were all equally subjected.   In China the customary law of the empire, while still the law under which the trader in the towns and the farmer in the villages both follow their vocations, has taken no such development as in England, and law is not paramount, nor are the emperor's ministers and servants subjected to it.   In Europe generally the administration of the law is now so equitable, and even in the Middle Ages was so open, that the people even then were not averse to calling it in to their aid.   In China, whatever the case may have been in a bygone golden age, the application of the law is to-day so uncertain, and its administration so much at the mercy of hidden influences, that the people shrink from appealing to it and prefer to settle their differences among themselves whenever possible.

These are some of the aspects suggestive of difference in the atmosphere in which gilds were organised and developed in both East and West, and, in the West, reached their decline; but there is one motive common to both, the desire to obtain advantages for one's self and to retain them, and at the same time to exclude others from their enjoyment. This was the prevailing motive in Europe during the Middle Ages, and down even into quite modern times,[1] and is in China to-day, coupled in both cases with the conviction that any benefit granted to another must *pro tanto* diminish the profit to one's self. China has not yet emerged from that state; and the fate which has befallen the great London companies, once so influential, but now shorn of all their power, is still, or so it appears, far removed from the gilds in China. These are as active and as effective as in the past; and the explanation given,[2] that they have remained so because they have not reached that accomplishment of their mission which has been reached by the gilds in Europe, only partially covers the ground. It is true that the mediæval conditions prevailing both in Europe and in China five hundred years ago, are still prevalent in China with but slight change, while in Europe they are so far altered that gilds are no longer needed for the protection of the merchant and the craftsman and the promotion of their special interests; but it is equally true that Europe no longer holds the opinion, once generally held, that trade is a stagnant pool, and that the abstraction of any portion of its content for the benefit of another is detrimental to one's own interest,

---

[1] Ashley, ii., p. 15; Unwin, p. 1. The powers of the English craft gilds were gradually absorbed into the municipality. In France, Belgium, and Holland the gilds were swept away by the French Revolution; they were abolished in Spain and Portugal in the period 1833-40, in Germany and Austria in 1859-60, in Italy in 1864.

[2] Unwin, p. 4.

while in China the people have not emerged from the state in which that view is held. When China's gilds shall be reduced to a stage of innocuous desuetude it will perhaps be because the social conditions have so much changed that their mission may be considered to have been accomplished, but it will also be because the gild members have formed an economically truer notion of the working of trade.

Another reason for the difference in the fortunes of gilds in the two quarters of the globe may perhaps be found in the dictum[1] that, "as soon as in any industry the amassing of great capital became feasible, as in the great London companies, the gild system tended to become a mere form." This condition has not yet been reached in China. Great fortunes derived from industry have been, and are, known there; but inquiry will show that they have invariably been made possible by the more or less direct connexion of the "merchant" with the bureaucratic world; the merchant has in such cases worked through the gild, but the gild has been his servant, subserving his interests in any direction that he might dictate. In general, apart from the official circle, which is drawn from the people but is armed with extraordinary powers, China is a country of great individual poverty, and of small accumulation of capital; the mere fact that, outside the radius of foreign influence, the ordinary rate of interest per mensem is but little less than the usual bankers' rate in London per annum, is a sufficient indication of this notorious fact.

[1] Ashley, ii., p. 169.

A further reason is the fact that, in China to-day, the law does not give the individual any adequate protection against coercion by the collective gild. During the Middle Ages in Europe the individual was affected by public opinion to an extent that we can hardly realise, and as the fellow-citizens of a merchant or craftsman were also members of a gild, the moral influences brought to bear on a recalcitrant member were of a kind such as we see manifested in connexion with a sympathetic strike to-day in localities in which trade unions may appear to dominate the law. The verb "boycott" is of modern coinage, but the thing has existed for centuries; and in former times the boycotted man was an outcast, not even solaced by the sympathy of a political party. In China these conditions still exist. Dame Rumour with her thousand tongues flies from tea-house to tea-house, and circulates exaggerated reports, many times worse than the fact, of the fate which has befallen, or is about to befall, an offender against custom, or one who would injure his neighbour. In Europe, however, the gildsman was also a burgess, and could appeal to the commune—the whole body of burgesses —to protect him from oppression by a portion only of the community. In China his only appeal for pro-tection is to his own gild, which is oppressing him; this is his only buckler against the tyranny of the officials, who are the "king's servants" but above the law, and who are never[1] natives of the town, or even the province, in which they exercise their functions. The Chinese gildsman has thus been debarred from transferring his activities to municipal

[1] Since 1912 under the Republic this ceased to be the rule.

government, in which he has had no share or influence,
and has been driven, if he would secure the protection necessary for his trading or his industry, to
increase the strength of his gild in every way. The
result is that he is helpless against this strength of
his own creating.

THE RELIGIOUS FRATERNITY

THE RELIGIOUS FRATERNITY

THE hanse or gild merchant, organised to retain the advantages of trading in the locality for the benefit of the denizens of the locality, does not exist generally in China to-day, nor, with two or three exceptions to be referred to later, is there anything to show that it ever has existed; but other forms of gild, such as that exemplified in the steel-yard, and in the craft or mistery, are both found there in full vigour. The gild, in its restricted sense of a solely religious and benevolent fraternity, also exists in China, under the name of Hwei, or "Association," the name also given to the secret anti-dynastic and revolutionary societies which have permeated the empire for a century past and more. These religious associations are formed to do honour to a designated demi-god or canonised worthy, as was the case with the early English trade fraternities, each of which was dedicated to a certain saint[1]. The English fraternities were formed to maintain chantries and buy masses for the dead and prayers for the living, and administer charitable funds, and to dine in connexion with both functions. The Chinese Associations have never bestowed alms or administered benevolent funds, and the subscriptions are devoted to making burnt offerings to their patron saint, and these offerings, having thus been sanctified, are then divided among the contributing members for their

---

[1] In the Appendix at p. 95 are given the Rules of the Carpenters gild of London, founded in 1333.

own consumption.[1]   The English fraternity seems to have been a stage generally precedent to the craft gild;[2] the Chinese Association appears never to have developed further, unless the religious side of the trade gild is an indication of such development in the past. The religious feeling of the West in the Middle Ages was intense, but the religious fraternity was made to subserve the business purposes of the gild to which it was affiliated; religion in China to-day creates no depth of conviction, and, perhaps for that reason, has no influence on the craft.

[1] Decennial Reports, 1892–1901, ii., p. 339.
[2] Ashley, ii., p. 74; Unwin, p. 52.

THE CRAFT GILD

THE CRAFT GILD

THE craft, or mistery, or company of Europe finds its counterpart in China in the trade combinations usually denominated Kung-so, literally " public office " or " public place," which may be explained as " the place for the consideration of matters of common (as distinct from private) interest." They are sometimes called Tang, "hall," which is also the usual designation of benevolent societies, such as those existing for the provision of free coffins, for maintaining soup kitchens, for the rescue of stray dogs, etc.

Origin.—The history of the English crafts can be traced nearly back to their origin, owing to the fact that they derived their powers from grants by king, parliament, feudal lord, or municipality, and at times were brought into political or fiscal conflict with one or other; and the records of the grants and of doings under them are accessible to the historian.

In China there are no original records of the past of any kind, except casual references in the old chronicles and an occasional inscribed tablet; and, with numerous devastating conquests and re-bellions, and an architecture worked generally in wood, there are few or no surviving muniments. Trade gilds have always been of purely democratic origin, without grant or licence from the governing powers; this has deprived them of the dignity which would entitle them to recognition by the serious

13

(Chinese) historian, and has driven them to secret methods, so much so that to-day it is not always easy to obtain copies of their regulations. The Chinese claim a venerable age for these organisations. The preamble to the regulations of the Druggists' gild at Wenchow declares that " from days of yore to the present " all trades have organised by making re-gulations, modified according to time and circum-stances.[1] The Bankers' gild of Ningpo refers the origin of its craft back to the establishment of the nine Bureaux of the Treasury of the Chow dynasty (B.C. 1122-255), and to the institution of different standards of currency in the Han dynasty (B.C. 206-- A.D. 25).[2]

Membership.—The aim of the English gilds was to include all workers in the craft, and, in their earlier policy, even to enforce membership on all, whether burgesses or aliens (*i.e.* craftsmen from other towns, English or foreign);[3] the later policy was to restrict membership by demanding that admission should be, at first, "upon the security of six reputable men of such certain mistery or craft"; then the assent of the " Wardens of the same trade " was required; then (in the case of the Drapers in 1364) it was ordained that " no one should use that mistery unless he had been admitted by the common assent of the same mistery";[4] then by the exaction of heavy fees from apprentices admitted to the freedom of the craft.[5]

In China there is no question of compulsion; the craftsman who is not a gild member is as one exposed

---

[1] Macgowan, p. 145.   [2] Ibid., p. 159.
[3] Ashley, ii., pp. 18, 75, 90.   [4] Ibid., p. 77.
[5] Ibid., p. 90.

to the wintry blast without a cloak. At the same time the existing members are by no means desirous of having competing craftsmen free from their collective control. The result is that membership is open to all of the craft on terms laid down by the gild, and that these terms are readily accepted.

Membership is generally limited to traders of the town, but in some instances we have the peculiar case of a craft gild of aliens excluding the townsmen; thus at Wenchow, in the province of Chekiang, the Fish-hook-makers' gild is composed solely of men from Foochow, the Needle-makers' gild solely of craftsmen from Taichow (in Chekiang) and from the province of Kiangsu, the Gold-beaters' gild solely of men from Ningpo; the men of Wenchow are rigorously excluded from these gilds, and it is even forbidden to give them instruction in the craft.[1]

Government.—In the early days of the English crafts the government was largely democratic; the feudal lord (in London the sheriff) appointed bailiffs to preside over the craft halimots and to collect the lord's tolls, but their authority was soon reduced to a formality, and the crafts became self-governing through their annual or biennial meetings and their weekly courts.[2] Then wardens were elected annually at full assemblies of the men of the craft, whose duty was to supervise the industry and cause offenders to be punished;[3] and with the custom of commuting the tolls for an annual payment,[4] and the duty of holding bequests in trust for the gild or religious fraternity connected with each mistery, these wardens developed into governing heads. Then on the

---

[1] Macgowan, p. 181.   [2] Unwin, p. 31.
[3] Ashley, i., p. 89.   [4] Unwin, p. 36.

institution of the incorporated company we have a strictly oligarchical government;[1] starting with a uniform body of a master and four wardens,[2] in time there grew up an advisory committee of usually twelve " assistants," ordinarily composed of past-masters and past-wardens.[3]

In China the gild government is, as might be expected, more democratic. The Tea gild at Shanghai has at its head an annually elected committee of twelve, each committee-man acting in rotation for one month as chairman, or manager; no gild member may refuse to serve on this committee.[4] The Bankers' gild at Ningpo elects annually a treasurer and a committee of twelve; the committee-men serve each in rotation for one month as manager, his principal duty being to act each morning as a clearing house.[5] The Carpenters' gild at Wenchow elects five headmen; these present a rare case of recognition by the officials of the city, certain corvée duties being demanded in return.[6] The Millers' gild at Wenchow is composed of sixteen mill proprietors, who select annually from their number a committee of four, in such way as to bring each gild member, in his turn, on the committee; but the ruling price of flour for each month is settled by the entire craft in conference.[7] In the gild government here indicated we have almost pure democracy, due partly to its complete dissociation from the government of the country, but more to the deep-rooted distrust of delegated authority or agency which is constant in every Asiatic mind. Another officer attached to

---

[1] Unwin, p. 217. [2] Ibid., pp. 158, 159, 161.
[3] Ibid., p. 219. [4] Macgowan, p. 152.
[5] Ibid., p. 160. [6] Ibid., p. 173.
[7] Ibid., p. 176.

the more wealthy craft gilds, the salaried secretary, will be referred to when we come to describe the provincial club.

Income.—The revenues of the crafts of England came from quarterage paid by all members, from penalties inflicted for breach of disciplinary rules (court fines, though inflicted by the gild, going to the city[1]), from voluntary subscriptions by the more wealthy members, and from the income from bequests.[2] The last was the most fruitful source of revenue, but income-producing property was ordinarily bequeathed to the religious fraternity connected with the craft, for the good of the testator's soul, the gain to the craft being a charge for management and some indirect benefits. In one case of a bequest, in 1515 to the fraternity of the Drapers' craft, of property calculated to produce £15 7s. a year, the income was distributed in this way: salary of chantry priest, £6 17s. 8d.; cost of yearly obit, 20s.; an almsman at 1s. a week, £2 12s.; coals for the poor, 1s. 8d.; potations for the drapers attending the obit, 6s. 8d.; priests and clerk of the church for ringing and for potations, 3s. 4d.; the mayor and sheriffs, 6s. 8d. each, the master of the Drapers, 4s., the four wardens, 3s. 4d. each, the clerk, 1s., the beadle, 4d., for attending the obit; remains to the craft, £2 7s.[3] The first three or four items in this account would be less likely than the last to benefit from any increment in the income derived from the property bequeathed.

The Chinese crafts have no such source of income

[1] Unwin, p. 41.
[2] Ibid., pp. 119, 123, 124, 221; Ashley, ii., pp. 90, 114, 153.
[3] Unwin, p. 207.

as pious benefactions, but none the less, while some
are very poor, others have large endowments from
the accumulated savings of years.   For example, the
Fishmongers' gild at Ningpo is reputed to have had
twenty years ago a reserve fund of $700,000 (then
equivalent to £125,000); for current income it
levies a tax, ultimately of course paid by the fishmongers and the consumers, on each fish-carrying
boat according to a published tariff; and each fishmonger, on joining the gild, deposits $3,000 (£550)
in the gild treasury, as a guarantee fund against
breaches of the gild regulations.[1]   The Druggists'
gild at Ningpo is reputed to have an annual income
of $500,000 (about £85,000), but the proportion of
income from endowments is not stated.[2]   The Tea
gild at Shanghai assesses its members a fixed sum for
each chest of tea sold by them, 4d. (in 1888) for black,
and 3d. for green tea; monthly account sales are
sent in to the gild, and the penalty for understate-
ments discovered by the gild audit is a fine of fifteen
times the difference; in addition there is an entrance
fee of $100 (£18) and a dinner of forty or fifty plates.[3]
The Bankers' gild at Wuhu seems to be supported by
a system of fines; each member deposits a guarantee
fund of 100 taels (£24), and this sum is the fine inflicted for the breach of several of the rules: for
giving or accepting a rate for changing money other
than the gild rate, or another than the gild rate for
drafts, or giving customers another than the gild rate
of interest, or for ante-dating or post-dating drafts,
or for doing business with a banker who has not
renewed his deposit after being fined, or for causing

---

[1] Macgowan, p. 171.   [2] Ibid., p. 140.
          [3] Ibid., p. 153.

loss to a fellow-gildsman by underhand dealing—
quite a Draconian code.[1]   Entrance fees are common.
At Wuchow the gild of Commission Agents collects
on admission a fee of 180 taels, the Bankers one of
40 taels, the Pawnbrokers one of 200 taels, the
Stationers one of 50 taels, the Opium dealers one of
100 taels; on the other hand, the Timber gild at
Wuchow collects no entrance fee, but levies a tax or
assessment of 1.60 tael (about 5s.) from each raft
passing the port; while, as examples of other sources
of revenue, the gild of Commission Agents collects
from the principal, for the gild funds, a commission of
0.5 per mille on the proceeds of sales; and the Opium
gild collects from the owner 2 taels (about 6s.) for
each basket of opium sold otherwise than through
members of the gild, and the latter will only sell
when, in their judgment, selling will not break the
market; and members are fined 100 taels for breach
of any of the gild regulations.[2]   In the Bankers' gild
at Ningpo the treasurer debits each member monthly
with an equal share of the month's expenses.[3]   On
the other hand, the Timber gild at Ningpo assesses
its members according to the amount of their sales,
averaging one-tenth per cent. on the turnover; an
audit is, as usual, provided by inspection of every
member's books by accountants of the various firms
detailed in rotation [4]—eloquent testimony to the
power of the gilds and the solidarity of the merchants
in .China.   These are some examples from some of
the wealthier crafts, but of the sources of income
of the poorer trades we have no certain knowledge;

[1] Decennial Reports, 1882–92, p. 289.
[2] Ibid., 1892–1901, ii., pp. 337–39.
[3] Macgowan, p. 160.   [4] Ibid., p. 139.

their income is presumably derived from " quarterage,"
equal monthly or quarterly dues from all members,
or in some cases from firms irrespective of the number
of masters and journeymen they may represent.

Common Worship.—The fraternities or gilds were in
England the nucleus from which, generally speaking,
grew the crafts or misteries.[1] The earlier fraternities
were essentially secret associations, and were formed
for all purposes, in the Middle Ages, when it was sought
to establish a social bond which should be at once
intimate, binding, and secret.[2] The religious feeling
of the Western world was strong, and such a feeling
provided a stronger bond of union than even trade
interest. We find accordingly that in every trade
was formed a religious fraternity, assumedly before the
formation of the secular mistery, but invariably found
in existence after the grant of a charter to a craft or
upon its incorporation as a company. Thus we find
that the Weavers' craft of London, chartered by
Henry II. (1154–1189), was authorised to "hold a
yearly gild in the Church of St. Nicholas Hacoun
on St. Edmund's day, to which all the mistery must
come on pain of a fine of 3d.;[3] and that the
Weavers' craft of Lincoln, also chartered by Henry II.,
was granted that "no one could exercise the craft
within twelve miles of the city unless he belonged to
the gild of the weavers of Lincoln, which was constituted in the name of the Holy Cross."[4] So, too,
there were the Goldsmiths' fraternity of St. Dunstan,[5]
the Tailors' fraternity of St. John the Baptist,[6] the
Skinners' "fraternity or gild in honour of Corpus

[1] Ashley, ii., pp. 74, 140; Unwin, pp. 4, 51–54.
[2] Unwin, p. 67.   [3] Ibid., p. 44.
[4] Ibid., p. 94.   [5] Ibid., p. 95.
[6] Ibid., pp. 95, 158.

Christi," [1] the Drapers' " gild in honour of the
Virgin Mary," [2] and numerous others, each connected with its own craft, each dedicated to its
own patron saint, and each attached to certain
specified church or churches. [3]

There is no such distinct evidence of any strength
in the common worship of the craft gilds in China. A
new member of the Druggists' gild at Wenchow is
called upon to pay an entrance fee to the treasurer of
the temple of the God of Medicine; [4] and, in the
Silk-weavers' gild of the same city, apprentices, when
out of their time, must pay the gild 1,500 cash (5s.)
for temple expenses, while new gild members must
pay twice that sum for the same purpose; [5] and many
gilds include among their minor penalties fines of
candles for the temple (so, too, in England, candles
and wax for the fraternity [6]). These are indications
pointing to the practice of gild worship in common.
It may be said that there is always craft connexion
with some temple. At Shanghai eighteen of the
poorer crafts, having no gild hall of their own, hold
their annual meeting in the City Temple, [7] to be
found in every Chinese city, and these meetings have,
of course, some religious observance as a part of
them. At Wenchow the Blacksmiths' gild announced
a new scale of wages and prices with the following
in the preamble: " We convened a meeting in the
City Temple, and, during the theatrical entertain-
ment and feasting, we agreed upon a new tariff of
wages for work and of prices for our wares." [8] This

[1] Unwin, p. 159.   [2] Ibid., p. 161.
[3] Ibid., pp. 107 *et al.*   [4] Macgowan, p. 145.
[5] Macgowan, p. 175.   [6] Unwin, p. 123.
[7] Decennial Reports, 1892–1901, i. p. 526.
[8] Macgowan, p. 172.

combination of religion, feasting, and strict business is customary in China, and was customary in the English crafts. An important function of the English fraternity, the setting forth of pageants,[1] forms no part of the religious side of the Chinese crafts, but the wealthier trade gilds furnish pageants —because of their wealth, and solely on the secular side. The main purpose of the English fraternity, to act as a benevolent society for relieving the poorer men and women of the craft, finds no counterpart in the Chinese crafts. The English fraternities were careful in attending the funerals of those of the craft, and in providing lights and masses,[2] the penalty for absence from either dirge or funeral being usually a fine of a pound of wax. In China it is a matter of pride for well-to-do families spend large sums on funerals, and customary for friends of the family to send contributions toward the expenses, much in the way that wedding presents are sent in the West; and the fellow-craftsmen of the deceased would be among the first to contribute. For poor members of the gild, contribution would always be made from the gild treasury, usually taking the form of a suitable coffin, and probably also of candles and offerings to the manes of the deceased.

Control of Trade.—In any comparison of the powers of the crafts in England and in China over their respective trades, we must always bear in mind the differences in the social environment. In England we have the crafts demanding privileges from their feudal lords, and later from king or municipality, and obtaining by charter the grant of specified rights.

[1] Ashley, ii., pp. 78–80; Unwin, pp. 95, 267 *seq.*
[2] Ashley, i., p. 92; Unwin, pp. 101, 118, 214.

These rights were, in effect, always a delegation of powers which, by both the theory and the practice of the time, were already inherent in the grantor. Taking the municipalities alone, the magistrates had full authority over markets, and determined at what times both burgesses and " foreigners " should offer their goods for sale; they also required dealers to display openly their entire stock, to prevent regrating and to allow to all a knowledge of the quantities offering.[1] Magistrates also had the sole privilege of tronage, or the right to establish public scales and to levy tolls for their use.[2] They had the right to restrict the " use " of a craft to those who enjoyed the freedom of the city, and to prescribe the conditions on which alone that freedom would be granted.[3] They also had the power of inspection, to see that none but wares of standard quality were offered for sale; and it was this power which, delegated to the crafts concerned, armed them with their most potent weapons.[4] The regulations of nearly all the crafts conform to a common type which may be represented by those of the Hatters, made in 1348, which were in effect: [5]

1°. Six lawful men to be sworn to rule the trade.

2°. None but freemen to make or sell hats.

3°. Apprentices to serve at least seven years.

4°. None to take apprentices but freemen.

5°. No night work.

6°. None of the trade to be made free of the city or to be allowed to work if not attested by the wardens.

---

[1] Ashley, ii., p. 19.   [2] Ibid., p. 20.

[3] Ibid., p. 76.   [4] Ashley, ii., p. 77; Unwin, p. 90.

[5] Unwin, p. 89.

7°. None to receive another's apprentices or servants if not properly dismissed.

8°. Nor to receive them if in debt to previous master.

9°. No stranger to sell hats by retail, but only wholesale and to freemen.

Under these powers granted to many, if not all, of the crafts, the fullest control was given over the trades, and foreigners' wares were often seized and destroyed on the ground that they were not up to the civic standard.[1] This was the period, the middle of the fourteenth century, when in many of the cities of Europe—Paris, Florence, Ghent, Cologne, London, and many others—the crafts wielded the whole power of municipal government.[2] Then set in a period of reaction, and, in England at least, of resumption by the municipality of its abandoned authority; and a century later an act of the English parliament prescribes that " whereas ... gilds ... make among themselves many unlawful and unreasonable ordinances, as well in prices of wares as other things," ... no new rules should be made for the government of a trade unless first submitted for the approval of the executive authorities.[3] In course of time the civic control thus resumed was either dropped in favour of individual initiative, or was assumed by the national authority.

In China the government is solely a taxing and policing organism, and its intervention in the affairs of the business world, in so far as it does not spring

---

[1] Unwin, p. 90; Ashley, ii., p. 77.
[2] Unwin, p. 61; Ashley, i., p. 85.
[3] Ashley, ii., p. 160; Unwin, p. 161.

from motives of personal profit to the officials, is
based on ethical principles, and not on economic or
business grounds.   The trade gilds have grown up
apart from and independent of the government;
they have moulded their own organisation, sought
their own objects, devised their own regulations, and
enforced them in their own way and by their own
methods.   Working thus without support or restraint from the government of the empire or the
city, the Chinese gilds could easily have remained
entirely without power; but, partly from the irre-
sistible dead-weight force of an Asiatic democracy,
partly because the agents of government are drawn
largely from the mercantile class, partly because the
gild is able to profit from the business instinct which
is so strongly developed in the official mind, and partly
because of the enormous impulsive power of a
mediæval form of public opinion and the development
of the boycott by centuries of practical use, the gilds
have in fact obtained an enormous and almost un-
restrained control over their respective trades.   To
classify all the forms of regulation of trades by means
of gild action would be impossible in a limited space,
and a selection is all that can be attempted.

Silk Gild at Shanghai.—The rules of this gild vary
so much from time to time, according to the exi-
gencies of trade, that it has ceased to print them.[1]
The significant fact here is that the gild can not only
make its own rules, but can modify them at short
notice, and still secure their enforcement.

Bankers' Gild at Shanghai.—The rules prescribe a
charge of 0.3 to 0.5 per thousand for cashing country

[1] Macgowan, p. 156.

cheques; fix interest on current accounts, rates
settled monthly in gild meeting; on advances on tea
and silk the interest is 0.5 per mille per diem; settle
the rate of change for paying customs duties; prescribe the method and fees for assaying silver; prohibit speculative dealings in dollars and bullion, and
enforce the prohibition, when it is to its interest as
a craft.[1]

Bankers' Gild at Ningpo.—For many years this gild
held two meetings a day to serve as a bucket shop for
fictitious dealings in dollars; twenty years ago the
gild put a sudden stop to the practice. The gild
rules provide for settling the rates of exchange for
dollars, interest to customers, and hours for de-
positing money.[2]

Bankers' Gild at Wuhu.—The rules provide for
settling daily the rate for changing money; for
settling for drafts the number of days after sight or
after date; for settling rates of exchange and of
interest; forbid ante-dating or post-dating drafts;
prohibit underhand dealing to the injury of a fellow-
member; and prescribe that, for breach of gild rules,
the persistent defaulter shall be expelled and boycotted.[3]

Tea Gild at Shanghai.—The rules prescribe the
rates for storage and insurance, conditions for advances to country buyers of tea, rates of commission
and interest on advances, the incidence and rates of
charges for packing, porterage, etc., and regulations
for samples. One rule, always enforced, and with no
redress by appeal to the courts, is significant of the
gild's power: " Pending litigation with a foreign

[1] Macgowan, p. 160.   [2] Ibid., p. 157.
[3] Decennial Reports, 1882–91, p. 289.

firm, members of the gild shall transact no business with the delinquent firm; relations are not to be resumed until the case is adjudicated." [1]

Opium Gild at Wuchow.—By the gild rules the non-member owner may not sell his own opium, under penalty of 2 taels (6s.) a basket; and if he wishes to keep his opium on his own premises for a few days, he must pay 0.3 tael (1s.) a basket for the privilege; commission is fixed at 2 per cent., and board at 0.12 tael (4½d.) a day is charged to non-member owners sojourning in the gild hall; broker allowed twenty-five days for settling account sales; gild advances money against opium at 0.4 per mille per diem (14½ per cent. per annum); the scale for weighing the opium is prescribed, and another scale for weighing the proceeds in silver; and it is stipulated that the gild is to be sole judge when the opium is to be put on the market. [2]

Druggists' Gild at Wuchow.—Among other rules common to many gilds, this gild has one of special interest. It is provided that, if A is indebted to B, and transfers his business dealings to C, the gild shall bring the three parties together for an amicable settlement, and that meantime A is prohibited from trading with C until he has liquidated his debt to B. [3]

Fishmongers' Gild at Ningpo.—The rules provide, among many other stipulations, that every fish boat coming in shall be reported to the gild, which, upon verification of the lading, will then affix its seal to the manifest; no member (and most certainly no non-member) would dare to buy a boat's lading of fish which had not been duly passed by the gild. [4]

[1] Macgowan, p. 151.   [2] Decennial Reports, 1892–1901, ii., p. 338.
[3] Macgowan, p. 145.   [4] Ibid., p. 171.

Millers' Gild at Wenchow.—The rules provide that the gild shall settle the price of flour monthly; that no member may give credit to any one in debt to another member; that no member may grind any but his own wheat bought by himself; that (as usual) the gild's measures are to be the standard; and that no abatement is to be made in favour of large customers.[1]

These selections are fairly typical of an infinite variety of forms of craft regulation. They vary in detail and in the nature of the points expressly provided for; but all Chinese trade gilds are alike in interfering with every detail of business and demanding complete solidarity of interest in their members, and they are alike also in that their rules are not a dead letter but are actually enforced. The result is a tyranny of the many over the individual, and a system of control which must by its nature hinder " freedom of enterprise and independence of individual initative." [2] It is a system, however, which suits the Chinese character and adds greatly to their commercial power; and while it may be true of Europe that " speaking generally, we may say that, in the late Middle Ages, the time had not yet come for the free play of individual enterprise," [3] it is certainly true of China that she will, even now, be slow to throw away the cementing agency of the gild.

Standard Measures.—In England the municipality was required to keep standards of weights and measures, and to enforce their general adoption. In China the government has never regulated or controlled the

---

[1] Macgowan, p. 176.   [2] Ashley, ii., p. 167.
[3] Ibid., p. 168.

operations of trade; but each craft gild and each provincial club prescribes the measures to be used, and keeps standards for the guidance of their members. In England there was at least one common standard within the limits of one municipality; in China, in any one city, there are in effect as many standards as there are gilds and clubs.[1]

Jurisdiction over Members.—It is in the basis of the authority conferring on craft gilds jurisdiction over their members that we find the greatest difference between the West and the East. In England the first exercise of jurisdiction appears to have been based on the commutation of market tolls for an annual payment by the collective gild; for example, the Bakers' gild of London as early as the year 1155 paid to the Royal Exchequer £6 a year as commutation for their tolls, and collected the funds in weekly payments of a farthing, a halfpenny, or a penny from the gild members; this necessitated joint action and jurisdiction, which they exercised in hallmoots held four times a year.[2]   The fishmongers at an early date " captured their hallmoot by silent permeation,"[3] holding meetings twice a year, which all members of the craft must attend on pain of the heavy fine of 21d. They also held a weekly court to settle disputes between London fishmongers, or in which foreign fishmongers were interested; and any case affecting a fishmonger could be withdrawn from the Court of Hustings at Guildhall and taken before the Fishmongers' hallmoot.[4]   The Weavers' gild of London was established by charter of Henry II., who granted

---

[1] "Trade and Administration of the Chinese Empire," chap. vi.
[2] Unwin, p. 36.   [3] Ibid., p. 37.
[4] Ibid., p. 38.

them " all the liberties and customs which they had in the days of his grandfather, and that none shall meddle with their craft ... except through them or unless he belong to their gild," and other charters were granted to other gilds by the same sovereign in precisely the same terms.[1] These gilds then claimed and exercised the right to have their yearly hallmoot and their weekly court for hearing craft cases, and to withdraw such cases from the sheriff's court to their own; they enjoyed the same privileges by right of charter as those descending to the fishmongers from the old folkmoot. This jurisdiction of the gilds resembles closely the private jurisdiction in the hands of the lords temporal and spiritual, which constituted so large a part of local government in the Middle Ages; [2] and, when exercised by the gilds, it has been called " collective lordship." This jurisdiction was, however, in all cases a delegation of a part of the powers of the superior authority—overlord or municipality. At the outset, while all regulations must be approved by the municipality, the gilds were ordinarily empowered to deal with petty disputes or breaches of rule by their members; and by encroachment more and greater powers were assumed by them until they came to claiming the right to judge all pleas connected with their craft; [3] even when such pleas were dealt with by the mayor, he generally called together a jury of the craft to settle the question.[4] In time municipal government gathered strength, and the municipal authorities assumed the powers which had been delegated by overlords, and resumed those which

[1] Unwin, p. 44; Ashley, i., p. 86.　　[2] Unwin, p. 42.
[3] Unwin, p. 28; Ashley, ii., p. 28.
[4] Unwin, p. 89; Ashley, ii., p. 27.

had once been in their own hands; and, in the end by the act of 1503-04, gilds are forbidden to make any rules prohibiting their members from applying to the king's courts.[1] In England the gilds, and their members, and their trades, were all brought within the law.

In China the gilds have never been within the law. They grew up outside it, and, as associations, have never recognised the civil law nor claimed protection from it. They are rarely recognised by the government, except when they take the farm of the proceeds of a tax upon the commodities dealt in by the craft; and they make representations to the government ordinarily through a sort of envoy, their secretary. They have developed as self-governing bits of democracy. Such jurisdiction as they exercise is of their own creation; and, not being delegated by a superior authority, there is never any question of control or of resumption. Their jurisdiction over their members is absolute, not by reason of any charter or delegated power, but by virtue of the faculty of combination by the community and of coercion on the individual which is so characteristic of the Chinese race. The method in which the jurisdiction is exercised is expressed in the rules of one gild as follows: " It is agreed that members having disputes about money " [and, in practice, any other] " matters with each other shall submit their case to arbitration at a gild meeting, where every effort will be made to arrive at a satisfactory settlement of the dispute. If it prove impossible to arrive at an understanding, appeal may be made to the authorities; but if the complainant resorts to the courts in the first instance, without

[1] Ashley, ii., p. 161.

first referring to the gild, he shall be publicly re-
primanded, and in any future case he may bring
before the gild he will not be entitled to redress." [1]
This rule is expressed in moderate language; a
similar rule of another gild is more direct in its terms:
" It is agreed that after a member of the gild, an
individual or a firm, has been expelled, all business
relations with him shall cease; any member discovered
to have had dealings with him, from sympathy or
friendship, shall be fined 100 taels." [2]   In effect, sym-
pathisers would also run the risk of being boycotted.
The penalties for breach of the rules or ungild-like conduct range from a fine of candles for the temple, or
a dinner of ten or a score or more plates, or a theatrical
representation in the gild-hall or the temple, up to
money fines of a considerable amount, and, in the last
resort, to the cessation of business relations, the con-
demnation to trading catalepsy or death, the boycott.
Besides those already referred to, it will be well to
describe briefly some of the more characteristic modes
of enforcing the jurisdiction of the gilds.

Tea Gild at Hankow.—In 1883 a long pending
dispute between the gild and the foreign merchants
came to a head, the gild complaining of the constant
use of false weights by the Europeans, and the latter
complaining of the constant false samples.   The
foreigners refused to accept the gild's suggestion for
a settlement, and combined to stop buying tea.   The
gild accepted the challenge and gave orders to stop
selling.   In the issue thus joined, the bilateral boycott,

[1] Macgowan, p. 141.
[2] It is uncertain if this gild was a craft gild or a provincial club,
but the rules relating to jurisdiction over members are identical in
the two.

the ever-united Chinese had the advantage over the ever-disunited Europeans and carried off the victory.[1]

Opium Gild at Ningpo.—In 1884 the gild farmed (or commuted) the inland taxes on opium in the Ningpo district of Chekiang, and, in order to bring the drug under its absolute control, decreed that importers, foreign or Chinese, should sell to none but its members. The foreigners protested to their Consuls, but the decree was obeyed. On this action the British Consul at Ningpo stated: " British merchants here have constantly assured me that, if any member of the gild attempted to deal with them except on such terms as the gild approved, and these would always include purchase at below cost price, he would be ostracised; and that, if any non-member ventured to similarly infringe the rules of the gild, although he could in no legal sense be bound by them, he would be subjected to such persecution, by means of trumped-up charges or actual personal violence, as these associations in China well know how to employ." [2]

Silkweavers' Gild at Wenchow.—Quarrels among members are to be settled by arbitration. In a small matter, the one in fault is to be fined in candles; for graver offences the fine shall be a concert or a play; but a dinner shall not be imposed as a fine in quarrels. For forming a partnership with a non-member for a less period than five years, the penalty is a play and a banquet. A member who entices another member's workmen away is fined a play.[3]

Goldbeaters' Gild at Soochow.—A member of the gild, in connivance with the magistrates, took for a

---

[1] Macgowan, p. 167; Decennial Reports, 1882–91, p. 169.
[2] Macgowan, p. 168. " Commercial Report by H.M. Consul on the Trade of Ningpo during the year 1884," p. 211.
[3] Macgowan, p. 175.

special purpose a greater number of apprentices than was allowed by the gild rules. As he was under the protection of the magistrates, the gild had to walk warily, but the word was passed around " biting to death is no murder." Gild members to the number of 120 each took a bite, no one being allowed to leave the place whose lips and teeth were not bloody, and the rebel against the gild was soon no more.[1]

Wheelbarrow Gild at Shanghai.—Much of the transport of merchandise through the narrow streets of the port of Shanghai, with its large trade, is done on wheelbarrows, of a special type, but having single wheels with narrow tires; the average number licensed in 1907 was 7,386. At the annual ratepayers' meeting in March 1897, the year's budget voted included an increase of the wheelbarrow monthly licence fees from 400 cash (10d.) to 600 cash (1s. 3d.), the avowed purpose being to limit the number. The barrow men refused to accede to the increase, and their gild decreed a riot, which duly came off on April 1st and 2nd. The riot assumed such formidable dimensions that the volunteers were called out, armed parties were landed from three men-of-war then in port, and order was restored with much difficulty. On the 7th the Municipal Council announced that licences would be issued at the old rate, thus restoring order and re-starting trade. This surrender to the mob excited indignation, and at a mass meeting of the foreign community it was voted that the increased rate should be collected at all costs from July—which was done without further trouble. The rate then imposed, 600 cash a month, has continued to be collected since.[2]

[1] Macgowan, p. 182.   [2] Decennial Reports, 1892–1901, p. 468.

Servants' Gild at Shanghai.—During the riot at Shanghai on December 18th, 1905, it is known to several then there that, as a part of the plan of rising, all house servants were to have left their foreign masters. The riot came off prematurely and the plans were not carried through; but servants stated to their masters that, if the signal had been given, they would, unwilling though they were, have been under the necessity of leaving.

The Chinese trade gilds establish rules and compel obedience to them; they fix prices and enforce adhesion; they settle or modify trade customs and obtain instant acquiescence; they impose their will on traders in and out of the gilds, and may even, through the measure known as the " cessation of all business," cause the government to modify or withdraw its orders; and their end, that of having the absolute control of their craft, is obtained by methods of which some are indicated above.

Journeymen.—In England early in the fifteenth century we find journeymen banding together, independently of the master's craft, and forming religious fraternities, partly for the edifying practice of their religous duties in fellowship, but also probably because, in such a fraternity, they could promote their worldly interests without challenging the attention of the authorities. After attempting to suppress them, the masters in their gild took steps to bring them under their own supervision, and to form of them a junior branch of the craft. They were still free to hold their own meetings for festivity or religion; they could subscribe their pence for mutual benefit, but in other respects they fell under the control of the wardens of the craft, and did not always keep the keys of their own treasury. In the end they yielded to the power of the gilds and lost all independent initiative, until in recent times their fraternities have been revived in the trade unions.[1]

In China the practice differs. Trading crafts often admit only one partner to represent a firm, but in industrial crafts masters and artisans are equally admitted to membership; instead of standing in hostile attitude to each other, they combine against society at large. Occasionally journeymen may have their own organisations, but generally, when they feel the need of combining against the masters, they do temporarily what their brethren in the West formerly did permanently—they have a meeting in a temple and form a fraternity, which then, when their object is accomplished, is forthwith dissolved. A strike for increase of wages is usually successful in China; the magistrate intervenes if it leads to serious disorder, which it is his main object to avert in his district; and, as the journeymen have lean purses, and are too numerous to pay otherwise, sc. in their persons, it is usually the masters who become anxious to settle the dispute before they attract the attention of the magistrates to the possibilities of plucking them. The journeymen, however, have a sufficiently wholesome fear of the possible consequences not to beware of entering into strife unnecessarily.[2]

Apprentices.—This, as a distinct class, was of slow growth in England, but from the early part of the

---

[1] Ashley, ii., pp. 108 *seq.;* Unwin, pp. 226 *seq.*
[2] Macgowan, pp. 170, 180.

fourteenth century, a tendency is manifest to demand a minimum period of service as apprentice, usually of seven years, before admitting any one to the freedom of the city and of the craft. Then later in the same century steps were taken to limit the number that one master might have; as first not more than he could maintain, or more than he could " keep, inform, and teach "; then, in the next century a more direct limitation of numbers, either one, or two, or three according to the master's standing in the craft, or else an apprentice to every two or three journeymen employed. The master's own children generally were excepted.[1]

In China we find the same control over apprenticeship. Many gilds rigidly restrict the number; some allow none but sons and nephews of gild members to learn the trade; the period of servitude varies from three to five years; generally speaking, no master may employ any one who has failed to complete his term of apprenticeship. The Silk-weavers-and-dyers' gild at Wenchow has rules which are very typical. In this gild it is ordained that—weaving is to be taught first, then dyeing; no shop may have more than one dyeing apprentice; a shop may have two weaving apprentices for every three looms; masters may have no more than one member of their own family learning the craft at one time; no instruction shall be given to any one not duly apprenticed; the term of servitude is five years, of which two are spent in learning to weave, and three in serving the master as weaver; when out of his time the apprentice shall continue to serve his late master as journeymen for two years; if the master does not wish his services, then only is

[1] Ashley, i., p. 89; ii., pp. 86, 91; Unwin, p. 91.

he free to go elsewhere; an apprentice may break his indenture, but in that case shall never again be admitted to the craft; apprentices are required to be respectful to journeymen.[1] These rules are in force in a trade gild in China to-day.

[1] Macgowan, p. 174.

THE PROVINCIAL CLUB

THE PROVINCIAL CLUB

THE second form of Chinese gild is the Hwei-kwan, " Club-house," sometimes, but not often, called Kung-so, the name generally given to the craft gild. It may be compared, in many of its attributes, to such associations of foreign merchants as the Steel-yard, the habitat in London of the merchants of the Teutonic hanse. The chief interest attaching to the Steelyard is not, however, in its internal organisation, but in the relations between it and the staple at which it was established, in the privileges granted to it and the restrictions imposed upon it by the authorities, national or municipal, of the trade area in which it did business; and comparison of the methods of the East and the West will better be deferred until we come to consider the European factories at Canton, and their relations to the government and the merchant gild of Canton.

The prime characteristic of the provincial club is that its membership consists entirely of officials and merchants foreign to the province in which it is situated, and to which they have been called by their official duties or by their business. It must be noted that the Imperial officials in China never exercise their functions in their native province,[1] and are always alien to the people under their jurisdiction; and that Chinese merchants reach out their trade tentacles in all directions, and, while settling freely in any of the provinces, never take root, but hold

[1] Cf. p. 5 note.

themselves in clannish seclusion apart from the natives of the place. It must also be noted that the provinces of China should be thought of as kingdoms of an empire, not as counties or circles of a kingdom; their relation to the empire resembles in one aspect or another that of Scotland to the United Kingdom, of Saxony to the German Empire, and of Kentucky to the United States; and the Cantonese is as much an alien in Shanghai as the Portuguese was in Spain when Philip II. was sovereign over both countries. When in an alien province, therefore, or even in some cases in another part of the same province, the Chinese early felt the need of combining for mutual support and protection, and this combination was effected through the agency of the Hwei-kwan, or Club.

Origin.—One club, in the preamble to its rules, boldly dates back to the mythical Emperor Shun (B.C. 2256-2208), who established uniform standards of length, weight, and capacity, and by whom triennial examinations were first instituted; he also ordered that the cane should be substituted for the severe punishments then in vogue in the schoolroom. Coming to historical times, it is probable that they were in existence during the Tang dynasty (A.D. 618-907); and early in the Ming dynasty (A.D. 1368) there is a certain record of a Kiangsu club at Peking.[1]

Membership.—All reputable natives of the home province are eligible for membership, though sometimes a firm may be represented only by its senior partner. All who are eligible must join, if they wish to do business in the alien province; sometimes a member who introduces a new arrival is paid a commission on the new member's contribution to the

[1] Macgowan, pp. 135, 150.

Club.[1] In the clubs in Peking the official element naturally predominates; in those in the provinces the greater number are merchants, since they stand most in need of mutual support. The clubs at Peking assist needly students, co-provincials, who come up for the Imperial examinations.

Government.—The provincial club is an encampment in hostile territory, and it must often have occasion to adopt an offensive defence; its government is, therefore, never so democratic as that of the craft gild, organised for operating in the home of the members. The government of the club is vested in a general manager, elected annually, but very commonly re-elected year after year; there is sometimes also an assistant manager; both these officers receive compensation, ranging from as little as six dollars (12s.) a year to a thousand dollars (£100) or more for the manager. There is also always an advisory committee, from three to twelve in number, serving usually without compensation, and elected annually, but eligible for re-election.[2] The most important officer of the club is the permanent secretary, a salaried scholar of literary rank. By his education he can conduct the club's correspondence with the officials in properly turned phraseology, with suitable telling quotations from the classics; and by virtue of his rank he has the entrée to all government offices without fear of being browbeaten, while his position as the spokesman of the club gives him a recognised standing. He is the medium of communication, and appears in court as the club's legal

[1] Decennial Reports, 1882–91, pp. 120, 158.
[2] Macgowan, p. 138; Decennial Reports, 1882–91, pp. 38, 120, 405; Decennial Reports, 1892–1901, ii., p. 334.

representative, pleading for its interests, demanding redress for its members, defending and protecting his constituents, and using his influence to get cases, in which the club or its members are interested, called from the national tribunals to a settlement by the club. The local authorities find him useful in soliciting from his club subscriptions for charities and extra-ordinary occasions.[1] The co-provincial officials serving in the alien province become members of the club and support its interests, but they take no share in its government.

Income.—The club derives the income needed for its maintenance and the promotion of its interests in exactly the same way as the craft gild, and what has been said of the one may be taken as applying to the other.[2] Two special points may be noted. In the rules of the Hanyang club at Ichang (an instance of a club representing another district of the same province) it is provided that members shall be assessed 0.3 per cent. on their trade, and that strangers (presumably temporary visitors) from Hanyang shall pay to the club treasury 3 per cent. on the value of any trade done by them.[3] The rules for the " Memorial Chapel erected in the Kiangnan (*i.e.* Kiangsu and Anhwei) club to canonised worthies from Kiangnan " at Chungking, while leaving the amount of the bene-factions of others subject to their own wish, stipulate that, when they visit the shrine for sacrifice, co-provincials who fill the official post of Taotai or Prefect shall contribute 4,000 cash (8s.) each, and that of Ting or Hien 2,000 cash (4s.) each for them-

---

[1] Macgowan, p. 138; Decennial Reports, 1882–91, p. 405.

[2] Macgowan, p. 139; Decennial Reports, 1882–91, pp. 38, 122, 158, 405; Decennial Reports, 1892–1901, ii., p. 334.

[3] Decennial Reports, 1882–91, p. 158.

selves and their retainers.[1]   In the clubs at Foochow
(and probably elsewhere) it is a general custom to
demand a contribution from a co-provincial who
comes to fill one of the higher posts. The Hupeh
club has the following tariff: Viceroy, 600 taels (£90);
Literary Chancellor, 500 taels (£75); Provincial
Treasurer, 400 taels (£60); Provincial Judge, 300
taels (£45); Taotai, 240 taels (£36); and Prefect,
200 taels (£30). From a Viceroy the Kiangsu club
demands 500 taels (£75); the Kiangsi club, 200 taels
(£30); and the Anhwei Club only 40 taels (£6).[2]

Common Worship.—What has been said of the
common worship of the craft gilds applies also very
closely to that of the provincial clubs, with one dis-
tinction. The club can hardly be expected to feel
any special reverence for the alien city temple, and
generally provides for worship in its own club-house.
When funds permit, this is usually done in connection
with provision for theatrical representation—an open
courtyard for the generality, galleries on both sides
for privileged spectators, the stage at one end and the
altar at the other.[3]   The altars are dedicated to minor
gods, such as the God of War, the Queen of Heaven,
or the Goddess of Mercy, or to canonised Emperors,
such as Yü the Great (†B.C. 2198) and Wu Tsung of
the Tang dynasty (†A.D. 847), or to canonised
worthies, natives of the home province.[4]   One important duty of the clubs is never neglected, that of
providing for the suitable burial of the dead. They
invariably have their own cemetery, in which they

[1] Decennial Reports, 1882–91, p. 122.
[2] Decennial Reports, 1892–1901, ii., p. 114.
[3] Macgowan, p. 139.
[4] Decennial Reports, 1882–91, pp. 120, 539; Decennial Reports,
1892–1901, ii., p. 334.

grant graves for their poorer members, in order that their bones may lie in ground which is a substitute for their native soil; and for them they provide coffins, either free or at reduced cost. They as invariably have a mortuary, in which may be deposited the coffined bodies of the wealthier members, waiting days, months, or years for the accomplishment of the desire of all Chinese, that their bones may be taken back for burial in their ancestral home.

Control of Trade.—The craft gild operates on the industry of a certain defined area, and within that area the conditions of Chinese life make it easy for the collective craft to exercise the most absolute control over all who " use " the craft, over the artisan who produces or the trader who sells and exports the product. The provincial club is designed to control the movement of trade, nominally that to and from the home province, although, in point of fact, there is no such limitation; and it is organised to push the individual and collective interests of the body of aliens who constitute its membership, and to protect those interests against the hostility of the natives and the extortion of the officials. The preamble to the rules of the Ningpo club at Wenchow declares: " Here at Wenchow we find ourselves isolated, mountains and seas separate us from Ningpo, and when in trading we excite the envy and hostility of the Wenchow traders, and suffer insult and injury, we have no adequate means of redress. Mercantile firms, if each looks only after its own interests, will experience disgrace and loss, the natual outcome of isolated and individual resistance. It is this which imposes on us the duty of establishing a club." [1]

[1] Macgowan, p. 136.

An application of the old illustration of the faggot of sticks. The control over those engaged in trading may be exemplified from the rules of the Hanyang club at Ichang [1] :

1°. Each firm pays to the club 0.3 per cent. of the value of its trade annually, the club auditing its books.

2°. Firms which subscribed to the erection of the club-house pay entrance fee 1.6 per cent. of their capital as shown in their books, and are then exempt from further payment.

3°. Members are taxed for boats they own or charter, 300 cash (9d.) [2] for each trip of a small boat, larger boats in proportion.

4°. Workmen pay 30 cash (¾d.) a month to the club; their employers, if not otherwise contributing, are also liable for a tax to the club.

5°. Clerks pay 2 per cent. per annum of their salary.

6°. Clerks starting in business on their own account pay 1,000 cash (2s. 6d.) for the right to a sign-board, in addition to the usual fees.

7°. Merchants opening a shop or office for the first time pay 2,000 cash (5s.) for their sign-board, and 1,000 cash (2s. 6d.) as entrance fee.

8°. New-comers of the workmen class pay 1,000 cash (2s. 6d.) entrance fee.

9°. Firms opening a branch have an additional fee to pay.

10°. Strangers from the home district must pay

[1] Decennial Reports, 1882–91, p. 158.
[2] In all conversions account is taken of the date of the authority quoted, the rate of exchange having varied greatly in the last thirty years.

the club 3 per cent. of the value of any trade done by them.

11°. Such strangers coming to sell cotton cloth pay 4 cash ($\frac{1}{10}$d.) on each large piece, and 2 cash ($\frac{1}{20}$d.) on each small piece sold.

12°. Members going into partnership with outsiders pay according to their share in the partnership.

13°. Any member first reporting the arrival of a townsman is paid one-tenth of the new-comer's contribution to the club.

14°. A member in default with his dues is dealt with. Any one giving support to a defaulter is fined.

These rules seem to provide a fine-meshed net to sweep into the club treasury something from every operation of trade. The control over these operations may be exemplified from a summary of the rules of the Shantung club at Ningpo : [1]

Credit.—All dealing to be in dollars [thereby eliminating the question of exchange between the Shantung tael of the club and the Ningpo tael of the locality]. Payment for grain in forty days, for oil and beancake fifty days, for goods in bundles sixty days, from date of bill of sale. Breaches of this rule entail on both seller and buyer a fine of a theatrical performance and dinner.

Delivery.—Free storage is allowed for no more than seventy days; after that storage must be charged. Delivery from ship within ten days. Fire risk on seller within five days of sale, after that on buyer.

New Year.—[All Chinese accounts must be settled on or before the last day of the year, unless otherwise

[1] Macgowan, p. 150.

provided for by a public authority; most clubs and most of the trading craft gilds forbid re-opening for business before the fifteenth day of the first month.] This club provides that goods sold in the tenth month are to be paid for on the twenty-fifth of the twelfth month, and those sold in the eleventh are to be paid for on the fifteenth of the second month of the new year. Sales in the twelfth month are to be reckoned as if made on the first of the second month in the following year.

Weighing.—Besides keeping the usual standard weights, the club prescribes that the ordinary sixteen-ounce-to-the-pound steelyard is to be the standard, and to be used by every firm belonging to it; that weighing is to be done in the presence of both parties; and that no claim for short weight can be entertained afterwards.

Fictitious buying and selling is strictly prohibited; offenders to be reported to the magistrate. Other offences are dealt with and penalties inflicted by the club.

There are other rules regulating the rate and incidence of charges for porterage, for packing, etc., etc., and settling the tare for various kinds of goods.

The provincial club exercises a control over its members and their trade, as absolute as the control of the craft gild, but with some limitations where the operations of trade are not entirely within the club, and these it is now necessary to examine.

Jurisdiction over Members.—In its jurisdiction in cases between two members, or when a member has contravened its rules, the provincial club is absolute. The Hu-Kwang (Hupeh and Hunan) club at Wuchow declares : [1] " The club is established to encourage fraternal relations between our fellow-provincials, and not for litigation or the adjudication of cases; but should disputes arise between members, the matter shall be laid before the club, and the president will give his decision on it after careful consideration. Any member who, without authorisation, ventures first to appeal to a court of law, shall be fined." In all probability he would be dealt with much more seriously than by a mere fine. In the rules of the Canton club at Wuchow, it is provided that, in the event of a dispute between two members, the complainant shall first pay the club 200 cash (6d.) for the expenses of a meeting; the president straightway adjudicates on the case in conjunction with the advisory committee; and, if his decision is not acceptable, he then allows an appeal to the courts.[2] So far all is clear sailing since the club is dealing only with its own members; but it has two other functions to perform of much greater importance— to protect its members from adverse action by the officials, and to support its members' interests against non-members—and in these two respects, unless the matter in dispute can be arranged by arbitration, which the Chinese would always prefer, recourse must be had to official or legal proceedings.

In disputes between members and traders of the locality or from a third province, when an amicable settlement is found to be unobtainable, an example of the mode of procedure may be found in the rules of the Canton club at Pakhoi. Therein it is provided [3]

[1] Decennial Reports, 1892–1901, ii., p. 336; Macgowan, p. 141.
[2] Decennial Reports, 1892–1901, ii., p. 334.
[3] Macgowan, p. 136.

that the club "undertakes to prosecute at law on behalf of its members, when satisfactory proof is produced of the equity of their claims. When a member has occasion to go to law to obtain redress for a serious grievance and finds his resources inadequate for prosecuting the suit, the club will, conjointly with the complainant, petition the court praying for an adjustment of the dispute; half the cost of legal proceedings in such a case will be defrayed from the club funds; but if it is found that the complainant has a bad case, or that his trouble has come from his irregular life, no claim for assistance will be entertained further. If a member goes to law to effect settlement of a money claim, the club will defray three-tenths of the cost of legal proceedings; but before the case is taken up, the unanimous consent of members present at a meeting called to consider it shall be obtained."

For action taken by a club to protect its members against harsh dealing and oppression by the authorities of the place, a characteristic instance is that of the Ningpo club at Wenchow just a hundred years ago, in the reign of Kiaking. There was then a scarcity of rice in the neighbouring provinces, while southern Chekiang had had an abundant harvest. Ningpo traders at Wenchow, under the general authority of an Imperial edict permitting the shipment of rice from any one part to any other part of the empire, chartered vessels for the purpose of exporting rice; but the local authorities, always desirous of preventing any increase in the price of food within their juris-diction, refused to admit the applicability of the edict to the existing conditions at Wenchow, and seized the vessels and placed the merchants under arrest.

The club, failing to obtain redress locally, appealed
to the higher authorities at Hangchow, the provincial
capital; failing in this appeal, they carried the matter
to the Imperial Government at Peking, and there
with the backing of their compatriots among the
officials of the central administration, the aggrieved
merchants had the justice they prayed for.[1]

The so-called " Ningpo Joss-house " riots at
Shanghai in 1874 and in 1898 afford an illustration
of the methods adopted by a provincial club, when it
finds its interests or those of its members injured by
the action of governmental officials or the hostile
attitude assumed by a large body of traders alien to
them. Of all the provincial clubs at Shanghai, that
of the men of Ningpo is the wealthiest and the most
influential; its club-house, a favourable specimen of
Chinese architecture, is situated in the French Settlement. At Shanghai the three (French, English, and
American) " areas reserved for foreign residence and
trade " are settlements, and not concessions, though
the French authorities have always called that under
their control " Concession Française." Within their
limits foreigners are permitted to acquire land by
agreement with the original owners, and to exercise
exclusive municipal authority; but the ground has
not been leased to the foreign government, as in a
concession, and the titles to property are issued by
the Chinese authorities. The property of the Ningpo
club had remained in its own control, but was of
course subject to the police, sanitary and road regulations of the government of the municipality in which
it was situated. In the spring of 1874 it was decided
to make two new roads through what was then nearly

[1] Macgowan, p. 137.

open country, running past two sides of the club-house, and both intersecting the club's cemetery, crowded with graves as close as they could lie. Of all the duties of a provincial club, that of providing the mortuary and the cemetery is held to be the most important; and any action affecting either adversely is most deeply resented, respect for the dead and the desire to rest in the home soil being most deeply implanted in the Chinese character. The club committee protested against the proposed violation of their consecrated ground, and, while undertaking to abide by any others of the municipal regulations, refused to consider any proposal to run roads through the cemetery in which lay the bones of so many of their compatriots. The municipality insisted on the letter of its rights, and the Chinese from Ningpo assembled in their thousands to assert the spirit of their rights. The riot which ensued lasted two days, entailed landing armed sailors from the ships of war and calling out the volunteers from all the Settlements to preserve the common peace, and resulted in the killing of eight Chinese and serious injury to many, foreign and Chinese. Peace was restored on the second day, May 4th, upon the French Consul-General entering into a formal agreement to respect the recognised rights of the club, and an undertaking that its cemetery should not be disturbed.[1] This settlement was confirmed in the most explicit terms by the French Minister in 1878.

In 1898 the club-house and its cemetery were surrounded by houses, and on sanitary grounds the municipal authorities decided that the mortuary and cemetery should be removed. They accordingly

[1] *North-China Herald,* May 10, 1874.

notified the committee of the club that they had decided to expropriate, at its assessed value, the ground occupied by the club's mortuary, with its included shrine, and by the cemetery, for the purpose of erecting a school and hospital for Chinese, and of continuing the street which ended at the cemetery wall. The club paid no attention to this *ex parte* notice, and on the due date the municipal authorities proceeded to raze the cemetery walls, having first taken the precaution to mass their police, to warn the volunteers of the Anglo-American Settlement, and to have men landed from the war vessels in port. The desecration of the cemetery aroused the Chinese to fury, and the scenes of 1874 were repeated. The riot which ensued lasted two days, resulting in the killing of upwards of twenty Chinese and injury to many others. While the riot was at its height the club decreed the " cessation of business " by all men of Ningpo—bankers, merchants, artisans, servants, stevedores, wheelbarrow-men, etc., etc.; the decree was generally obeyed, and the trade of the wealthy port of Shanghai was held up for several days. In the result, the agreement of 1874, confirmed on 1878, was upheld, and the club remains in undisturbed possession of its mortuary and cemetery.[1]

[1] Decennial Reports, 1892–1901, i., pp. 469, 524.

THE GILD MERCHANT

THE GILD MERCHANT

Of the gild merchant, organised by the entire body of merchants of a locality, to regulate the trade of the locality and to divert its course to their own benefit, there are only three well-marked instances in the history of gilds in China.

THE GREAT GILD OF NEWCHWANG

The membership of the Great Gild is composed of the principal Chinese bankers and merchants of the port of Newchwang. From each of the two divisions of the town, the Eastern and Western, are elected annually a president and a vice-president, constituting a committee of four, who govern all gild matters. The duties assumed by the gild may be divided into two categories. As an unofficial municipality it performs duties which, in China, are consistently neglected by the constituted authorities: maintains streets, drains, and reservoirs; controls the common lands; relieves the poor; maintains or supports charitable societies, etc. As a gild merchant it draws up and enforces regulations for the control of banking, markets, trading, etc.[1]

The income required to provide for the expenses of the gild are derived from fees levied on the trade of the port, of which the following are typical:

1°. On all trading operations between (Chinese) merchants not belonging to Newchwang, $\frac{1}{10}$ per cent.

[1] Decennial Reports, 1882–91, p. 34.

2°. Bridge dues, 8 cash (¼d.) for each cart carrying fuel, and 16 cash (½d.) for each cart carrying other commodities.

3°. Annual dues from members, divided into eight classes, of which the highest pays 1,000 tiao [1] (£25) a year.

The presidents for the year are often required to pay for the honour by disbursing considerable sums from their private funds.

The gild's control over trade may be exemplified by the following sets of regulations drawn up at various times.

Regulations for the Assay of Silver

1°. The standard for silver is 992 fine, and no one shall cast ingots of another fineness.

2°. A premium of 1.5 tiao (about 0.27 per cent.) is allowed on each 50-tael ingot of silver 1000 fine brought to be remelted.

3°. For each 50-tael ingot a charge of 2 tiao (0.36 per cent.) for Tientsin, Shanghai or Fengtien silver 992 fine, and of 1.5 tiao for Kirin silver.

4°. Silver of 998 fine, coming chiefly from Chihli and Shantung, to be taken at par; but on lower grades, less than 998 and more than 992, a charge of 1.5 tiao for each 50 taels.

5°. A charge of 32 cash (about 2 per cent.) per tael on Kulow silver in small lumps 992 fine.

6°. For other and inferior silver, the charge to be determined by the degree of fineness.

7°. No banker or assayer is allowed to cut rates,

[1] The tiao, elsewhere of 1,000 cash, or, in North China, of 1,000 nominal=500 actual cash, in Newchwang contains 1,000 nominal=160 actual cash.

nor to impress his die on any ingot not cast by himself.

8°. Charges not provided for above to be settled by agreement between the parties.

9°. Penalties, 1 per cent. of the value of the silver involved.

Rules for Exchange Transactions

1°. A commission not exceeding 2 per cent. may be charged by bankers on all moneys passing through their hands on account of non-members; and the banker shall guarantee the quality of the silver paid out.

2°. All exchange transactions are to be conducted in open market, but, during the hours the exchange is closed to public business, bankers will be allowed to negotiate bills for sums not exceeding 100 taels.

3°. The money market shall be open only to members of the gild, and to such merchants from other towns as have been introduced by a member. Visitors, however, shall not be allowed to bid in the market, and all their business must be transacted through a member.

Rules for Regulating the Grain Market

1°. A stone pillar has been erected to mark the eastern limit of the grain market; any one buying grain outside this limit will be fined 100 tiao (£2, 10s.), and similarly buying fuel or straw 30 tiao (15s.).

2°. Carters (*q.v.* vendors) altering on their contract notes (actually on the thill of the cart) the price agreed upon by the merchant for their cartload, shall be fined 10 tiao (5s.) if carrying grain, and 4 tiao (2s.) if carrying fuel or straw.

3°. Any one trying to break a bargain between a carter and a merchant, as by offering higher prices, shall be fined 30 tiao (15s.).

One method of regulating the trade of the port in the interest of the gild members is peculiar to Newchwang, and, in decribing it, it is necessary to use the past tense, since the influx of foreign interests and the general introduction of foreign bank-notes since 1900, and more especially since 1905, has worked a great change, and probably relaxed the grasp of the gild on the trade of the port. A merchant selling imports, nominally for cash, was, unless he was willing to submit to a discount of from one to five per cent. according to the market rate, compelled to accept payment in "transfer money," *i.e.* by cheque, giving him a credit at a bank. Specie, too, in the place was attracted to the banks by the offer of a premium ranging from 0.2 to as much as 6 per cent., and could be withdrawn only on quarter day, four times a year; withdrawal was discouraged by crediting the account quarterly with premium, if not withdrawn, at the same rate as if deposited. During the deposit, while the money could not be withdrawn, cheques could be drawn against it for "transfer" to the account of another, not necessarily at the same bank. Exports, too, could be bought only with "transfer money"; and all quotations for drafts on other places were in terms of transfer money. Except for copper coinage, there never was money in Newchwang outside the banks, members of the gild; and aliens were driven to take in goods for export the proceeds of sale of their imports, and always through the agency of members of the gild. No one had cash to offer, except at heavy cost, and no one was in a position to act independently, even if the Great Gild had been as weak as it was strong, and if it could be imagined as permitting what, in fact, it never did permit.

THE SWATOW GILD

Swatow itself is an unimportant place, with a population estimated at 65,000, and a trade in 1907 valued at 45,000,000 taels (£7,250,000). The people of the country and coast around are, however, industrious workers and hardy fishermen, and the merchants are adventurous traders, whose influence is felt in every port along the coast. The people are exceedingly clannish, and to injure a Swatow man is to plunge the hand into a nest of hornets. The trade of the port is absolutely, in its minutest detail, under the control of the " Swatow Gild," the Wan-nien-feng (" Prosperity for a myriad years "), and the Swatow men in other ports are as completely organised in provincial clubs, working in conjunction with the home gild and under its guidance.

The home gild, though a fighting body, is under a government which in form is very democratic. It is divided, territorially, into two divisions, each of which elects annually twenty-four firms as representatives, making a committee of management of forty-eight members. The routine business of the gild is managed by four clerks, nominated by four members of the committee, two from each division in rotation, the four serving as accountants and treasurers for one month. In important affairs the committee is advised by three secretaries, one to represent each of the divisions, and the third being the salaried literate secretary, whose qualifications and duties have been described in connexion with the provincial clubs. While the government is thus democratic, in practice a question affecting any branch of trade is first discussed among the principal firms whose interests are touched; having come to an agreement, the smaller firms concerned are taken into their council; and when all are agreed, then the matter is brought before the gild. At the gild meetings there is seldom any discussion, and if there is likely to be much opposition to the proposed measures, the matter is withdrawn. In the more serious questions, especially where the government is concerned, there is no debate and no record; and, if there seems to be a general feeling that the matter should be proceeded with, it is left to the prime movers to take the necessary steps, strong in the knowledge that they have the full power of the gild behind them, and yet able to maintain all the secrecy of private initiative.[1]

Of the Swatow clubs, that at Chefoo may serve as type. The government is in the hands of a committee formed by a representative of each of the leading firms, six to eight in number. The committee men take turn in assuming the presidency for one month each. The committee seldom meets, and the president of the month acts in all matters on his own initiative, but he does not often disregard the wishes of the firm which may, at the time, be of the greatest importance. The club has also a literate secretary.[2]

The income of the home gild is provided by taxes on the trade of the port according to a tariff as elaborate in some ways as that of a custom-house, including

[1] Decennial Reports, 1882–91, p. 537.   [2] Ibid., p. 77.

fees on steamers, sailing-vessels and junks, owned or
chartered by members, payable on each entry of the
vessel; and taxes, either per package or *ad valorem*,
on about fifty enumerated categories of goods. Money
fines are not mentioned; any member absent from the
festival of the Queen of Heaven, the patroness of the
gild, is fined 10,000 fire-crackers; the same penalty
is inflicted for non-attendance at a special meeting.[1]
The income of the club at Chefoo comes from a
similar taxation of the members' trade, but it is
provided that under-declaration is to be punished by
a fine of ten times the amount sought to be evaded—
a provision apparently not needed in the home gild.[2]

The duties undertaken by the gild are so broad in
their nature that they may be summarised in a few
words. It concerns itself with the commercial interest, individual and collective, of its members;
enacts and enforces rules regulating trade; performs
many of the functions of a chamber of commerce, a
board of trade, and a municipal council. It supports
a fire brigade, levies its own taxes, provides standard
weights and measures, fixes rates of commission,
determines settling days, provides penalties against
frauds and tricks of trade, and acts generally as the
guardian of the interests of its members and the terror
of all who would injure them.[3]

When the gild wishes to enforce its decrees, there
are no inflammatory placards and no riots; it would
seem almost as if an aura pervaded the minds of
members of the gild, leading them, without pre-
concert, to do the same thing at the same time in the
same way. A steamship company, in order to close

---

[1] Decennial Reports 1882–91, p. 539.
[2] Ibid., p. 78.   [3] Ibid., p. 538.

a loophole for possible fraudulent claims, inserts a
clause in its bill of lading without previous consulta-
tion with the gild. A few friendly, very friendly,
hints are given, but there is no formal protest; only
merchants, apparently without reason, cease to ship
by the steamers of that company; a sugar refinery
at another port, under the management of the same
firm, suddenly remarks a serious falling off in its orders;
and when the loss in all directions has assumed serious
proportions, the hint is probably taken and the ob-
noxious clause struck out of the bill of lading. A
steamship company, the same or another, refuses to
pay a claim for damaged uninsured cargo, holding
that the damage was properly a subject for insurance;
this may happen once or twice, without more than a
protest from the firm directly concerned; but if it
happens repeatedly, no matter how much the company
may be in the right by its own national law, the
gild takes action. There are no lawsuits, not even a
reference to arbitration; the company finds its freights
falling off, and is soon brought to view that class
of claims with a more lenient eye; it assumes the
insurance which once it held the shipper should have
provided, and does not even attempt to pass it on by
adding to the rates of freight.

In 1881 the customs at Swatow imposed a heavy
fine on some merchants for breach of a customs rule
relating to the examination of cargo. The merchants
felt themselves aggrieved, and the gild supported
them. The import and export trade of the port
came to a sudden standstill, and it was intimated,
by no one in particular, that it would not be resumed
until the grievance was redressed. In this case, not
dealing with the weak backbone of a Chinese official,

but with the foreign control of the Maritime Customs, the gild did not gain its point; but it persisted for fifteen days, during which time the external trade of the port absolutely ceased.

In 1890 the provincial authorities imposed a new tax on trade, to which the people of Swatow objected. Special agents were sent from Canton, the provincial capital, to collect it; but when they arrived at Swatow, no dealer in the taxed articles offered to pay the tax, or even to commute it; the agents could find no one willing to rent them premises in which to establish their office; and ultimately they returned to Canton, carrying the tax law back with them unenforced.

THE CANTON CO-HONG AND FACTORIES

In the trade between China and Western nations, from 1757 down to 1842, Canton was the " staple "; the " Thirteen Firms," commonly called the Co-hong, corresponded to the gild merchant, or hanse, as closely as the differences between the social conditions of the East and the West would permit; and the foreign factories were forced, long after the institution had disappeared from Western Europe, to assume many of the attributes of the branch of the hanse stationed for trade in foreign parts, which it will be convenient to designate as the Steelyard, the name given to the Teutonic hanse in London.

" The staple was an appointed place to which all English merchants were required to take their wool and other staple commodities for sale. Its purpose was to bring merchants so closely together that trade might be more easily regulated and supervised, and, especially, in order that the customs duties might be more easily levied. . . . We cannot, indeed, help seeing that fiscal motives largely prompted the various regulations, and that the power of removing the staple . . . was valued by the sovereigns as a useful weapon of diplomacy." [1] The English staple was at first placed abroad, usually at Bruges, frequently at Antwerp, sometimes at other towns; then several towns in England were selected, and foreign merchants were forced to come to England to buy; then on the conquest of Calais, that town was selected as being both abroad and in English territory, and it remained the staple permanently. With place-names changed, this description applies closely to Canton.

The Portuguese were the first to enter into the China trade, in 1516, and they traded at various places along the coast—Lampaco, Canton, Amoy, Chinchew, Foochow and Ningpo; they conducted themselves arrogantly, and, after the great slaughter of them at Ningpo, they settled in 1557 at Macao, which then, and down to 1848, was under Chinese territorial and fiscal control. The Spanish were the next, first visiting China in 1575, but their carrying trade they left to the Chinese trading with Manila. The Dutch came in 1662, and, after attempts, first on Macao and then on the Pescadores, settled to trade in Formosa; driven from there in 1662, they traded at Amoy and Foochow, and later at Canton. The first English ships arrived at Canton in 1635; in 1677 they traded also at Amoy, but were unable to obtain a permanent footing at Canton until 1684, owing to the jealousy and bribery of the Portuguese at Macao. The French, Americans and other nations did not enter the China field fully until the eighteenth century. During the

[1] Ashley, i., p. 111.

seventeenth century the small trade done was carried on at many points, but it tended to gravitate to Canton, partly because of the keen business instinct of both officials and merchants at that city, and partly because it was found that elsewhere the officials aimed at securing as many golden eggs as they could in the shortest possible time; and from the first years of the eighteenth century Canton was a self-constituted staple. With the curious inversion of Western practice, so often seen in the East, it was not the government which threatened to change the staple, but the foreign traders, whenever they found the extortion at Canton assuming what might be called unreasonable proportions, even for those longitudes. Finally in 1757 an Imperial decree prohibited foreign trade elsewhere than at Canton, and that city remained the staple until the treaty of Nanking in 1842 opened four other staples.[1]

In considering the relations between the Co-hong and the Europeans in the factories, it will be convenient to limit our purview to the English factory, since its affairs were under complete control, viz., that of the East India Company, since its trade was greater in volume than all the others together, and since it was in the forefront of the battle in the constant disputes on questions of trade, law and government. Before entering upon the Canton scene, we must first, however, see what were the conditions governing the merchant gild and the Steelyard in England during the Middle Ages.

The gild merchant, or hanse, was a society formed primarily for the purpose of obtaining and maintaining the privilege of carrying on trade—a privilege

[1] "The Trade and Administration of the Chinese Empire," chap. ix.

which implied the possession of a monopoly of trade in each town by the gild brethren.[1] It existed in every town in England—except London and the Cinque Ports—down to those that were not much more than villages; and a noted lawyer of the twelfth century held that the commune, *i.e.* the body of citizens with rights of municipal self-government, was identical with the gild merchant.[2] London seems to have had none, but its municipality, established at an early date, possessed all the rights which would have been conferred by a grant of gild merchant.[3] The government of the gild was in the hands of an alderman and two or four wardens or échevins, generally assisted by an inner council of twelve or twenty-four. The membership included all traders in the town, and did not exclude craftmen as such, and their rights could be handed down to sons, and even to the husbands and sons of daughters; and merchants from other towns were also admitted to membership. The regulations made by the gilds to control trade illustrate the spirit of the time, that, while members could push their own interests, they still must act in the common interest, and that all were bound to submit to regulations for the common good, and to come to the assistance of their fellow-members; for example, if a gildsman of Southampton were put into prison in any part of England, certain of the gild officers were bound to go at the cost of the gild to procure his deliverance; and, by the rules of many of the gilds, any member present could demand a share in a bargain. The jurisdiction of the gild had for one of its chief purposes the maintenance of the gild privileges. There are frequent

[1] Ashley, i., p. 71.   [2] Ibid., p. 72.   [3] Unwin, p. 60.

ordinances against acting as agents for the sale of goods belonging to non-members, or instructing strangers in the secrets of local trade; but, on the other hand, it was held to be of the greatest importance to maintain fair dealing and a high standard of quality.[1]

The foreign trade of England, during the time of the supremacy of the gild merchant, was largely in the hands of foreign traders,[2] and especially of Italians, who were the bankers and most unscrupulous usurers of the time; and frequently at the larger ports the actual owner, or farmer, of the king's custom was an Italian or a provost of Aquitaine, who worked hand 'in glove with the importers.[3] The import trade was not carried on by isolated individuals, but the merchants from a particular town clung together and sought privileges to be enjoyed in common. In those days " the merchants of, let us say, Amiens formed part of that body of burghers that governed Amiens; they were regarded as representing the interests of Amiens; their treatment depended on particular treaties with or conditions granted to Amiens, and, in any difficulty, it was to the magistrates [or merchant gild] of Amiens that they would look for assistance," [4] as we have seen illustrated in the case of the men of Southampton. In the English port the foreigners found themselves face to face with a body organised in the same way as that from which they were delegates, and for the same object—that of reserving as large a proportion of profit as should be possible. For this purpose many restrictions were imposed on the foreigner in the interest of the

[1] Ashley, i., pp. 73–76.   [2] Ibid., p. 103.
[3] Atton and Holland, p. 12.   [4] Ashley, i., p. 103.

burgesses of the town, without whose consent, as many
of the charters expressly stated, no one who was not
a burgher could carry on trade within the town.[1]
The restrictions imposed on non-burgesses varied
considerably, but we may distinguish several fixed
points:

1°. Strangers were subject to tolls from which
burgesses were partially or wholly exempt.

2°. Strangers were not permitted to buy from or
sell to other strangers, except under rigid conditions.

3°. Strangers were not permitted to sell goods by
retail, nor to go inland with their wares.

4°. Strangers were compelled to " go to host,"
i.e. to abide in the house of a burgess assigned to
him as his " host " by the gild authorities or the town
magistrates; the purpose of this was that every
transaction of aliens should be subject to the closest
scrutiny in the interest of the natives. On the
continent of Europe this restriction was rigidly enforced, but there was much laxity in England, greatly
to the discontent of the burgesses of English towns.

5°. The residence of foreign merchants in England
was limited to forty days.[2]

The fourteenth century was a period of alternate
victory and defeat in the battle between the foreign
merchants and the English traders. On the one side
was the sturdily independent burgess demanding the
enforcement of what he held to be his just rights.
On the other were the barons, whose interest was in
unrestricted trade, and the king guided by his fiscal
interest, to wit, the increase of the customs and the
easier negotation of loans from the foreign merchants,

---

[1] Ashley, ii., p. 12.   [2] Ibid., pp. 13–16.

who were the only bankers of the time. The privileges of London were in the hands of the king, Edward I., from 1285 to 1298, and in these fourteen years the restrictions against foreigners were generally relaxed. The reins were then tightened; but in 1303 the king issued the Carta Mercatoria, in which, in return for the payment of additional customs, he abolished all the previous limitations as to the time and place of residence, and as to the persons to whom goods might be sold, and permitted to foreigners the retail trade in spiceries and merceries; an interesting approach to the extraterritoriality enjoyed by foreigners in China since 1843, is found in the provision that in all suits between natives and aliens, one-half of the jury should consist of merchants, fellow-townsmen of the foreigner. From 1311 the burgesses were able to re-impose the old restrictions, but they were again relaxed in 1322. After another period of strictness, they were again relaxed by Edward III. in 1335, again in 1343, and again more completely in 1351. In 1377 [1] Richard II. granted a charter to London, under which all the old restrictions were imposed, without exception. In 1381 the foreigners' privileges were restored and the London retailers' monopoly was cancelled; then ensued the Great Revolt of Wat Tyler. In 1384 the restrictions were again imposed; and in 1393 came the final settlement, enduring to the end of the Middle Ages, and, indeed, far into modern times, forbidding aliens to deal with one another or to engage in retail trade.[2]

[1] It was at this time that Geoffrey Chaucer was Collector of Customs for the port of London, being controller of the custom and subsidy of wool, fells and hides, from 1374 to 1386, and controller of the petty, or alien's, custom from 1382 to 1386.

[2] Ashley, i., pp. 106–108; ii., pp. 13–19; Unwin, pp. 137–151.

In Canton we find a close parallel to what, as we
have seen, was the position of the English gild merchant, and of the oligarchic civic administration which
succeeded to its duties and privileges; and to the
restrictions imposed on the alien trader.   The differences are mainly such as spring from the different
social and political conditions.   In Canton the gild
was the creation, *ad hoc,* of the government, working
as one man and with all the forces of the government
behind it and was not composed of a numerous body
of freemen striving for the interests of the town and
of themselves; the fiscal interest of the emperor and
the members of the administration, at Peking and at
Canton, was not facility in negotiating loans, or even
the increase of the customs, but it was that the foreign
trade should be milked, and that the takings from it
should be both large and not subject to audit; and
the foreign merchants in the factories had the status
of a " Steelyard " thrust on them, and, filled with a high
appreciation of the might of the Chinese empire, they
had no thought, until the very end, of resisting the
restrictions which were imposed upon them.   The
restrictions took another form, but their nature was
the same, and they were more effective in accom-
plishing their object.

By the beginning of the eighteenth century, the
foreign trade in China had gravitated to Canton.
There it was subjected to many restrictions and
many exactions, but there was no consistent regulation, and loopholes were provided in plenty· by the
possibility of making private bargains; in fact, it was
the common practice for ships to stop outside the
Bogue, the entrance to the Canton River, until the
supercargo had gone to Canton and settled by nego-

tiation the amount of fees which his ship must pay. The first step in regulation was taken in 1702, when one merchant of Canton was appointed to be the sole broker through whom all foreigners must buy their teas and silks, and must sell the few foreign products for which a market then existed. This appointment of the "emperor's merchant" was objectionable to the foreign traders, because he could not supply them readily with a cargo; to the other merchants of Canton, who were shut out from a profitable trade; and to the officials, both territorial and fiscal, because he was the direct nominee of the emperor, and while exacting, as a matter of course, all the trade would stand, reported his collection only according to the moderate official tariff of the empire. Owing to this opposition, the emperor's merchant agreed to allow other merchants to share in the trade on payment to him of 5,000 taels (£1,667) for each ship but otherwise no concession was made to the foreign traders. From certain articles which were agreed to in 1715 between the supercargoes of the East India Company and the Hoppo (the Controller of Customs for the port and province of Canton), but which produced no lasting effect, we may learn what were some of the grievances from which they already suffered, and which they hoped to remedy. They included—unrestricted trade with all; liberty to engage and dismiss what Chinese servants they wished, while their English servants were to be left to the supercargoes to deal with; liberty to buy provisions and necessaries for their factory and ships; liberty to re-export unsold goods free of duty; that the Hoppo should "protect them from all insults and impositions of the common people and mandarins,

who were annually laying new duties and exactions
which they were forbidden to allow of"; that the 4
per cent. be taken off, and that every claim or demand
the Hoppo had should be demanded and determined
the same time with the measurement of the ship.[1]
These were, one and all, grievances of which a beginning had been made, and from which foreign
traders continued to suffer for over a century to come.

The last article given above requires some explanation. The 4 per cent. charge (on the value of
sales and purchases) dated from 1702; one of the
four was a gratuity imposed for the benefit of the
intermediaries (interpreters and others), and the
other three were for the Hoppo's staff. The " claims
and demands " were indeterminate and importunate.
The first was the measurement charge, for which, on
the Company's ship *Defence*, in 1689, the sum of
2,484 taels(£830)was demanded, but 1,500 taels(£500)
accepted; the ship measured " 94 coveds " (110 feet)
from before the mizzen-mast to abaft the foremast,
and " 23½ coveds " (27½ feet) in breadth, and the
limitation to the measurement for length is an illustration of the delightful system of " give and take "
which prevails in all cases of unregulated exaction.
Ultimately the extra-legal charge, as a consideration
for consenting to measure, came to be a customary
sum of 1,950 taels (£650) over and above the measurement fees proper. Other charges also grew up and
became stereotyped, and with them we shall have to
deal later; but monopoly and exaction had begun,
though, as yet, they were not fully regulated. Regulation was, however, soon to come.

In 1720 the merchants of Canton resolved to

[1] Auber, p. 153.

form themselves into one body, or Co-hong. This "combination which the Chinese were forming to set their own prices on the goods to be sold Europeans, thereby to have their proportions of the real profit on the said goods, whoever appeared to be the seller," [1] was essentially, except that it was limited to a few among the many merchants of Canton, an embodiment of the gild merchant; it purported to be an organisation of the merchants themselves, but, from the evidence of the strong grasp which the officials had on the foreign trade, it is beyond doubt that the company was formed with, at least, the support of the agents of government.

In 1727, as a protest against the continuous increase in the exactions at Canton, the supercargoes collectively threatened to transfer their trade to Amoy, but the Hoppo at once acceded to their demands. In 1728, in addition to the usual impositions, none of which had, of course, been actually withdrawn, an additional duty of 10 per cent. was imposed on all goods sold by the merchants, the charge naturally following the goods and falling ultimately on the foreign traders; the supercargoes appealed for redress, but without result, first to the Viceroy,[2] and then to the government at Peking. In 1732 the supercargoes ordered all the ships to remain outside the Bogue, until they should receive an assurance that their privileges would be respected; their demand was acceded to. In 1734 they attempted to obtain redress for their complaint on the quality of silks

---

[1] Letter of Court of Directors of East India Company to their supercargoes. In Auber, p. 156.

[2] The Viceroy, throughout Auber's narrative of events, is regularly referred to as the Isontock. This can only stand for Tsongtŭk, the Cantonese form of Tsung-tu, Governor-General or Viceroy.

and on irregular impositions also " as to the 1,950
taels "; [1] and again threatened to transfer their trade
to Amoy. In 1736, by an act of grace on the accession
of Kienlung, the 10 per cent. surtax was abolished,
in consideration of which " considerable presents
were made to the Isontock." In 1737 " renewed
but ineffectual efforts were made to obtain a remission of the 1,950 taels." [2]

The exactions continued to increase, and in 1747,
and again in 1752, special efforts were made to obtain
the remission of "the 1,950 taels" and other charges
enforced contrary to the Imperial edict of 1736; and
in 1754 steps were taken to open trade with Ningpo.
It was in 1754 that orders were given that every vessel,
on arriving, should be " secured " by two members
of the Co-hong, before negotiations would be begun
for settling the amount of measurement fee, gratuity,
brokers' and interpreters' fees, customs duties, lighter-
age charges, ship chandlers' charges, pilotage, etc., etc. [3]
This was a distinct step ahead in the strictness of
control over foreign trade; before this date the
Co-hong had a monopoly of buying the goods brought
by a ship, and of providing her with tea, silk and
other products for a lading outwards; but now every
operation connected with a foreign ship was to be
in their hands.

In 1757 an Imperial edict made Canton the sole
staple for foreign trade, and prohibited all traffic
outside that port. After an attempt at protest made
by sending their interpreter, Mr. Flint, to negotiate
at Amoy and Ningpo for trading facilities, [4] the

[1] Auber, p. 162.   [2] Ibid., p. 163.
[3] Auber, p. 168; Eitel, p. 6; Gutzlaff, ii., p. 90.
[4] Auber, p. 170; Eitel, p. 6; Davis, i., p. 57; Williams, ii., p. 448.

East India Company had to acknowledge defeat, and the fruits of victory were reaped by the officials and merchants of Canton, in the formal chartering of the Co-hong in 1760. Protests continued to be made, however, and in 1760 the Court of Directors of the East India Company sent to Canton a special representative, who formulated his demands for redress on the following points:

1°. The 1,950 taels.

2°. The 6 per cent. on imports and the 2 per cent. on all silver paid the Hoppo.

3°. To be allowed to pay their own duties, and not through the merchants who are styled securities, whom they charged with applying it to their own purposes.

4°. Direct access to the Hoppo, and direct access for appeals to the Viceroy.[1]

Fifty years later the foreign traders would have been glad to have so short a list of grievances.

In 1771 the Co-hong was dissolved by order of the Viceroy. "It cost Puankhequa 100,000 taels (£33,333) which the [East India] Company repaid him."[2] The reason assigned was that many of the firms composing the Co-hong were bankrupt and in arrears with the contributions due to the officials.[3]

In 1782 many Cantonese merchants were found to be heavily in debt to foreign traders, especially to natives of India, who had lent large sums to Chinese, attracted by the high rates of interest ruling in China.[4]

---

[1] Auber, p. 174; Gutzlaff, ii., p. 105.

[2] Auber, p. 178.   [3] Eitel, p. 8.

[4] "After Manho" (banished to Ili for bankruptcy) "left Canton, I saw in the hands of one of the foreign contributors" (to a compassionate fund for his benefit) "his promissory note for $60,000 bearing interest at 5 per cent. per month. This was not exorbitant, under the circumstances in which it was given. The current rate of interest, with the best security, was 1 per cent. per month on

On representations being made, an Imperial edict was issued, ordering that the debts should be forthwith liquidated by the general body of merchants, and prohibiting the incurring of such debts in future; and, as a guarantee for the future, the body of, at first " The Twelve," subsequently " The Thirteen Merchants," was chartered, to assume sole control of foreign trade, to ensure due obedience to the orders of the government, and to serve as the sole intermediary for communications between the government and the foreign traders.[1] This was, to all intents and purposes, the old Co-hong; but, instead of the old joint and several responsibility for all events and liabilities, they were given the administration of a Consoo (Kung-so, " gild ") fund, provided by direct contribution from the foreign trade, and available to meet any liability for debts, fines, impositions, etc. The gild merchant was now fully established.

In this brief historical résumé we have seen a merchant gild in the making under the mediæval conditions from which, notwithstanding her privileged East India Company, England had already emerged. We have now to study such a gild in the working, under conditions of almost unchecked authority.[2]

This gild, the Co-hong, operated in close touch with the agents of government, receiving their full support on the one hand, and on the other serving as the channel through which was transmitted the stream of wealth in which the officials expected to share largely; and, while we need not enter upon the questions of jurisdiction or the attitude of lofty supe-

running account, while 2 to 3 per cent. per month on temporary loans was common." Hunter, p. 39.

[1] Auber, p. 182; Eitel, p. 8.

[2] For this study in detail the reader is referred to the author's *Chronicles of the East India Company Trading to China.*

riority assumed by the Chinese empire, it will be well to describe briefly the functions of some of the officials who could exercise an influence on foreign trade.

The *Hoppo* [1] (in Chinese Kwan-pu), Controller of Customs for the port and province of Canton, received a direct Imperial appointment, and was quite independent of the Viceroy and other territorial officials, except in so far as he might require the arm of the law to help in the exercise of his functions within their jurisdiction. His functions were threefold: he had to collect the moderate sum at which his office was assessed for customs duty, and to maintain the numerous staff by which it was collected; he had to collect further and much larger sums with which to gratify the court and ministers at Peking, and to placate the high officials in whose jurisdiction his work lay; and he had to collect still further sums with which to reimburse himself the amount his appointment had cost, to buy a peaceful retirement, and to leave himself the fortune for the acquirement of which he had taken office. Adherence to a fixed tariff and exact report of his collection would have defeated the most important of these objects, in fact those which alone had any real importance in the eyes of the Chinese official world; and the Co-hong, in its full development, was the instrument by which he tapped the foreign trade to an extent, not fully realisable, but unparalleled since the palmy days of the Roman Empire.

The *Viceroy* (Tsung-tu or Chih-tai) of the two provinces of Kwangtung and Kwangsi had his official residence in those days at Shiuhing, some fifty miles

---

[1] Hoppo from Hoi-pu, truncated form in Cantonese of Yueh-hai-kwan-pu, Controller of the Maritime Customs of Kwangtung.

up-river from Canton, but was often at Canton at critical times. He was supreme in civil matters within his jurisdiction, except for the independent jurisdiction of the Hoppo, and was ultimately responsible for maintaining law and order. After a century of experience it was found that the easiest way of keeping the foreign traders in a proper state of respect for the law, as laid down by the officials, and for their orders, was through the Co-hong, and that body was now the inevitable buffer in all matters of dispute.

The *Governor* (Futai, styled Foo-yuan in the older books) had jurisdiction over the province of Kwangtung. During an interregnum, or in the absence of the Viceroy, he appears as his substitute.

Without enumerating the duties of the intermediate officials, Provincial Treasurer, Provincial Judge, Prefect (Kwangchow-fu) and others, at the foot of the scale we have the *Hien*, who is the primary agent of the government in collecting all taxes except customs and gabelles, is at once police superintendent and magistrate, and combines many other functions. We are concerned with three: two at Canton, the Namhoi and Punyü (the foreign trade at Canton and Whampoa lying within the jurisdiction of the latter), and the Heungshan Hien (in whose jurisdiction lay Macao, which, it must always be remembered, was under the fiscal control of the Chinese government).[1]

Among the many regulations made and added to from time to time, the following are the most important:[2]

1°. Ships of war must remain outside the river, and must not enter the Bogue.

---

[1] Ljungstedt, p. 10; Martin, i., p. 371; ii., p. 19.
[2] Auber, p. 344; Hunter, p. 28.

This rule was never relaxed. When warships arrived measurement fees were demanded, invariably in the eighteenth century, occasionally even in the nineteenth, and were usually rejected, but sometimes complied with.

2°. Women must not be brought to the factories; nor could guns, spears, or other arms.

This rule was rigorously enforced. As late as 1831 the Chinese threatened to stop the trade in order to enforce the immediate departure of three ladies who had come from Macao to visit the English factory.

3°. Hong merchants must not be in debt to foreigners.

Owing to the high interest, there was temptation on both sides for foreigners to lend money to Chinese; in 1831 it was ordered that these debts be liquidated within three months; this was done, but by the treaty of Nanking in 1842, the amount of such debts due eight years later, in 1839, was taken as being $3,000,000 (£650,000).

4°. Foreign traders must not engage Chinese servants.

This was regularly relaxed, but was always a weapon to be used *in terrorem.*

5°. Foreigns must not use sedan chairs.

Walking was the only method of progression suitable for foreigners, and not too much of that, since they were forbidden to leave the factories except under escort.

6°. Foreigners must not row for pleasure on the river. Three days in the month (on the 8th, 18th, and 28th) they might take the air, in small parties under the escort of an interpreter, who was held responsible for all their misdeeds.

This requires no comment.

7°. Foreigners must not present petitions; if they have anything to represent, it must be done through the Hong merchants.

> This required them to complain of any irregularity through the agent committing the irregularity, with no appeal, and from this rule there was no relaxation.

8°. "In the Hong merchants' factories where foreigners live, let them be under the restraint and control of the Hong merchants. The purchase of goods by them must pass through the hands of a Hong merchant; this was originally designed to guard against traitorous natives misleading them and teaching them. Hereafter the foreign merchants dwelling in the Hong merchants' factories must not be allowed to presume of their own accord to go out and in, lest they should trade and carry on clandestine transactions with traitorous natives."

> Foreigners must "go to host"; there was no necessity to forbid their trading with each other, but they must not trade, wholesale or retail, with, practically, any but their host.

9°. Foreigners must not remain at Canton out of season, but, their goods sold and their ships laden, must return home or go to Macao.

> This corresponded with the forty days' limit in England. For a consideration paid to the proper persons, permission could be obtained, under various pretexts, for two or three to remain behind in each factory after the general exodus. Though the annual departure was

compulsory, it, as well as the arrival, had to be paid for, the usual charge on departure being 300 taels (£100).

These were the more important of the regulations restricting the action of the foreign traders. Under them, in so far as they were merchants, and not super-cargoes coming in their ship, they paid for and obtained a permit to proceed from Macao to Canton in advance of the arrival of their ships; these must come before the end of the south-west monsoon (before the end of October), which would bring them safely and speedily the length of the China Sea from the Straits of Sunda or the Straits of Malacca to Canton. On their arrival in Canton, their first business was to select and arrange with their security merchant, who must be one of " The Thirteen Firms," and who was personally responsible for every act of the foreign traders, or their ships, or their crews. To enable him to accept that responsibility, the foreign traders were, without possibility of protest, placed in his hands. Foreigners must sell to him alone the goods brought in their ships; they were not under compulsion to sell—they were free to send the goods back in the ship—but they must sell to no one else. They must also buy from him the tea and silk for lading their ships outwards; here again they were under no com-pulsion—they need not load a cargo—but they must buy from no one else. They might go, three days a month, a-pleasuring to the flower gardens, but they might not walk freely in the street a hundred yards from the factories, to see what articles were in demand and at what prices they were sold; nor had they any means of ascertaining what were the just prices for the teas and silks they bought, since there was no competition. Their ships laden and away while the north-east monsoon still had strength to waft them down the China Sea, the traders must then pay for and obtain a permit authorising them to return to Macao, there to await the return of the next season.

The regulations affecting the traders' business— their ships and their lading—were as minute.[1] On the arrival of a ship at Macao, the first duty of her master or supercargo was to take a licensed pilot from the office of the Tso-tang, the deputy of the Heung-shan Hien stationed at Macao, to control and tax foreign trade at that port. Here too at first, but later at Whampoa, in the jurisdiction of the Punyü Hien, he engaged a ship's comprador (ship chandler), who had the sole privilege of supplying the ship with provisions and all other necessaries. Arrived at the Bogue, the ship must then be measured and obtain a permit to enter the river and proceed to Whampoa. An authentic account [2] of the fees paid officially for one ship of small size (420 tons) in 1830, shows the extreme elasticity of the tariff, over and above the gratifications paid to numerous subordinates to facilitate the smooth running of the machinery:

	Taels.
Tonnage dues calculated according to measurement of length and breadth .	842.285
Loss in converting into bullion . .	75.806
Shroffage	15.161
Official gratuity	810.691
Carry forward . .	1,743.943

---

[1] Hunter, *passim*. "The Trade and Administration of the Chinese Empire," chap. ix.

[2] Hunter, p. 100. See also Gutzlaff, ii., pp. 89–91.

Brought forward . .	1,743.943
Hoppo's " fee for opening the barrier " .	480.420
Transport to Peking and weighing in government scales	150.145
To the Superintendent of the Treasury .	116.424
Add 1 1⁄10 per cent. converting into bullion	1.280
Difference in weights between Canton and Peking, 7 per cent. . . .	174.455
Total . .	2,666.667 Taels.

These figures are already reduced by one-fifth, as for a " second-class " ship, but the total was equivalent to £900. In 1830, it may be noted, "the 1,950 taels" exacted as a gratuity from the large ships of the East India Company was reduced to 1,600 taels, consequent upon a resolution to send all the Company's ships away to Manila.[1]

During her stay of, usually, three months at Whampoa, the ship continued to give a steady stream of profit to the privileged ship's comprador and the privileged bumboatmen, and to the minor officials from daily and monthly fees, from payments to subordinates, and from numerous and uncertain gratuities to facilitate her working and expedite her departure.

The agent at Canton took the ship's manifest, giving full particulars of her lading, and handed it to his security merchant, and had no further concern with her inward cargo. As the security merchant provided office, storage and lodging accommodation, found servants for the foreigner and guaranteed them, and conveyed the imports from ship to warehouse in privileged (monopoly) lighters, so too he bought the imports at a price which he was able, or willing, to give, counting on selling them again at a price to

[1] Auber, p. 324; Gutzlaff, ii., p. 91.

allow a margin sufficient to cover his profit and expenses, all duties and charges claimed by the government, and the heavy exactions demanded by the officials. The East India Company stated that their net loss on British products shipped from England to Canton had been £1,668,103 in twenty-three years,[1] due, as the Company declared, to " forcing the trade beyond the demand," but as readily explainable by the absolute power given to the members of the gild merchant of Canton to fix prices themselves, with no check from free competition; even had the monopolists been willing to foster trade by giving better prices, they were not free agents in the matter, since they were under compulsion to provide a large margin between their buying and selling rates.

The imports having been thus disposed of, the foreign traders' next concern was, with the proceeds and with the specie which every ship then had to bring, to buy a lading outwards for their ships. Shipments of silk were, by law, limited to 167 cwt. for any one ship, and the demand for miscellaneous products was restricted; and outward cargoes consisted mainly of tea. This, too, as well as other exports, could be bought only from the trader's own security merchant. The foreign traders had, however, an option by custom—they could, at the close of a season, settle both quantity and price for the following season, or they could settle the quantity only, leaving the price to be determined by the rates ruling at the opening of the next season; but, whether they settled the price now or next year, it was with their security merchant that they had to settle it. In exports, also

[1] Evidence before Lords' Committee, 1820, quoted in Crawfurd, p. 24.

the Co-hong was under compulsion to provide a large margin between their buying and selling rates. Moreover the whole trade of any one ship was in the hands of one middle man, practically reducing it to a trade by barter, apart from the specie introduced; and if, by a refusal to buy, a stand were made for lower prices for tea, it was always open to the security merchant to adjust the equilibrium by giving lower prices for imports. As Burke declared,[1] comparing the monopoly of the Co-hong to the monopoly of the East India Company: "As the Chinese monopoly is at home, and supported by the country magistrates, it is plain it is the Chinese company, not the English, which must prescribe the terms."

The Chinese monopolists were at home, and they were supported by their officials, but for this support they had to pay; that was, in fact, the reason for their existence. The English king, in earlier days, found it to his advantage to foster foreign trade, and to break down the barriers which circumscribed the foreign traders and restricted their liberty of trade; it was from the foreign traders he could obtain loans and increased revenue from customary dues. The Chinese emperor wanted no loans—not for a century or two to come—and the gain to the fisc from customs dues was a bagatelle compared with the gains to individuals from levies outside all tariffs; and these gains, by the revised system dating, in its final shape, from 1782, came through the agency of the Co-hong. In them all at Canton had a share—Hoppo, Viceroy, Governor, and so on, down to Hien—with the secretaries, accountants, messengers, boatmen, servants, door-

[1] Ninth Report of Select Committee of House of Commons, 25th June, 1783, quoted in Crawfurd, p. 36.

keepers, etc., etc., of each one. Of them all the
Hoppo was chief, since he was master of the foreign
trade, and, in those days of slow communication,
foreign traders acted on the assumption that they
must conform to the laws, however enacted and however enforced, of the countries to which their trade
called them. As we have seen, the Hoppo had to
extract his millions from the trade; and, as his word
was law, he had no difficulty in doing it.

The Co-hong system worked with little friction.
The foreign traders enjoyed the practical monopoly
assured to them by their distance from the home
market and the difficulty of communication; they
paid nothing directly in the way of duties or charges,
except their contributions to the " Consoo " guarantee
fund, and had nothing of the extortion thrust under
their eyes; and the discomforts of their life, shut up
in rented quarters in the factories, were as nothing
to the prospect of accumulating a competency. The
members of the merchant gild, the Co-hong, were
bled, one way and another, to the tune of millions, but
could recoup themselves many times over; and the
Chinese officials were quite contented. The best
commentary on the commercial aspect of the system
is the admitted fact that there grew up side by side,
during a century of joint working, a body of Chinese
and of foreign merchants, than whom there has never,
at any time, or at any place, been a more honourable;
with never a written contract, with many an occasion
of help in time of difficulty, and with much sympathy
and friendliness from the one to the other. And yet,
all this was paid for by the foreign traders. That the
Co-hong system allowed the foreigner not only to
make a living but to accumulate a modest fortune,

that a member of the Co-hong should, when occasion
called for it, wipe out the debt of a foreign merchant
who had fallen into difficulties,[1] says much for the
generosity and the business capacity and foresight of
the Chinese merchants, but it emphasises also the fact
that there must have been a wide margin of profit to
allow of such liberality. For the Co-hong was the
"milker" of the foreign trade, milking it all it could
stand, and paying heavily for the privilege. As much
as 200,000 taels (£66,667) must be paid for a seat in the
gild; [2] contributions of 50,000 or 100,000 taels must be
made at frequent intervals for a Yellow River flood or
for purchase of official rank for a son; when the Chinese
debts to foreign traders were paid off in 1831 one
member contributed $1,100,000 (£245,000) and others
in proportion; and to the ransom of $6,000,000 for
the city of Canton in 1841 the same member contributed $1,000,000 (£225,000).[3] Notwithstanding
these heavy claims, this member, Howqua, himself
stated in 1834, nine years before his death, that he
valued his estate at $26,000,000 (nearly £6,000,000),
a great fortune for those days, probably the largest
mercantile fortune in the world; and this was the
surplus, after meeting the demands of numerous
" blind mouths "—officials who made the law, and
interpreted the law so made.

In the first third of the nineteenth century, the
foreign trade of Canton had gravitated to the English
race. The trade of the Portuguese, the Dutch, the
French, the Spanish, and others, had been reduced
to insignificant proportions; [4] and it may be said

---

[1] Hunter, pp. 42–44, 107; Nye, p. 40.
[2] Hunter, p. 36.   [3] Ibid., pp. 45, 47.
[4] Auber, p. 338; Hunter, p. 22.

generally that two-thirds of the entire trade was in the hands of the English, and one-fourth in those of the Americans. In the season 1836-37, for example, the trade was distributed as follows: [1]

BRITISH: Number of ships, 171.
    Value of imports (including 27,746 chests of
        opium, excluding treasure) . . . $34,435,622
    Value of exports (excluding treasure) . . 25,339,284
AMERICAN: Number of ships, 96.
    Value of imports (including 451 chests of
        opium, excluding treasure) . . . $3,214,726
    Value of exports (no treasure) . . . 9,527,139
FRENCH: Value of imports (including 100 chests of
        opium) $116,456
    Value of exports 138,547
DUTCH: Value of imports (including 10 chests of
        opium) $526,032
    Value of exports 1,070,290

In that same season the foreign residents in the factories at Canton were divided among the various nationalities as follows:[2]

	Firms.	Men.
British	31	162
Parsee	11	62
American	9	44
Portuguese [3]	1	28
German	1	4
Dutch	1	3
Swedish	1	2
Danish	—	1
French	—	1
	55	307

[1] *Chinese Repository*, Oct., 1837. The value of American exports has been increased to make the cost of tea per lb. correspond to that of shipments by British ships.

[2] *Chinese Repository*, Jan., 1837.

[3] The Portuguese (Macanese) generally occupied inferior clerical positions in firms of other nationality.

These figures all tend to demonstrate that the trade was in the hands of the British—from England and from India—and of the Americans.

The English were divided into two categories. On the one side was the East India Company, having a statutory monopoly [1] of the entire British trade, and actually monopolising that with England. On the other, were the " country merchants " (English and Parsee) trading in " country ships," under the licence, and subject in all matters to the control, of the East India Company—but their operations were strictly limited to the trade between Canton and India; they could import opium (value in 1836-37, $19,471,238) and raw cotton (value in 1836-37, $8,225,513), and they could ship tea and silk to India, but they were absolutely shut out from the trade with England.

The Americans, whose previous connexion with the tea trade had been through the East India Company by way of Boston Harbour, first entered into the Canton trade in 1784 with one ship. They were the " free-traders " of the day, in the sense in which the word was then understood; in America there were no privileged corporations, the trade was open to all on equal conditions, and the merchants and sailors of Boston, Salem and New York asked only a fair field and no favour. They soon assumed a leading position in the crowded factories of Canton, and the contrast between the opportunities open to them and to the equally enterprising and able " country merchants " under the British flag was galling to the latter in the extreme.[2] An agitation was begun in

[1] The " Chinese Monopoly " of Crawfurd's pamphlet.
[2] Auber, p. 323; Matheson, *passim;* " British Relations," *passim;* " Facts Relating," etc., *passim.*

England, in 1834 the monopoly of the East India Company was abolished, and Lord Napier was sent out as Chief Superintendent of British Trade in China, to put commercial and other matters on a proper footing. The question of the equality of nations was thereby brought to the front. This the Chinese stubbornly refused to admit, and insisted that commercial matters should be treated on commercial lines. They were quite satisfied with the existing situation, and saw no reason for changing it.

The position of the American traders had raised the question, but the English, though with some vacillation, carried it to a settlement single handed. War ensued, and the treaty of Nanking, signed August 29, 1842, provided in its fifth article that—" The government of China having compelled British merchants trading at Canton to deal exclusively with certain Chinese merchants called Hong merchants (or Co-hong), who had been licensed by the Chinese government for that purpose, the Emperor of China agrees to abolish that practice in future at all ports where British merchants may reside, and to permit them to carry on their mercantile transactions with whatever persons they please." The second article also provided for the opening of four additional ports to foreign trade, thereby depriving Canton of its position as the sole staple.

Thus ended the omnipotent gild merchant of Canton, smitten by the power of belligerent traders from the West; but the merchants of China, driven back upon their entrenchments, have continued the battle with the silent and more effective weapons of the craft gild and the provincial club. With these institutions of China to-day, institutions which disappeared as living realities from England with the Middle Ages, the Chinese have maintained their own in what would, without them, have been the hopeless contest of modern knowledge and procedure against the antiquated methods of the past.

APPENDIX

RULES OF THE GILD OF CARPENTERS, LONDON, A.D. 1333

Taken by permission from *A Book of London English*
By R. W. CHAMBERS and MARJORIE DAUNT
(Oxford: The Clarendon Press, 1931)

GILDA CARPENTAR) LONDOÑ

[Thi]s is þe boke of ordinaunces of þe brotherede of Carpenteres of Londoñ made [on þe] first day of Septembre in þe
ȝer of þe Regne of ouꝛ Lord Kyng Edward the [third]e after þe
Conquest vij

[In worschepe] of ouꝛ Lord ihꝰ crist & of his moder seint
Marie, & in þe name of seint Jo[sep & of seint] Johñ Baptist,
þe gode men Carpenteres han ordeined a Fraternite to be hold[en
in þe] chirche of seint Thomas of Acoñ be-syde þe Conduyt
of Londoñ, & in þe chirche of seint Johñ Baptist of Haliwelle
by-syde Londoñ, þat is to witen for to fynde a tapur brennyng
in certeyn tymes to·foꝛ oure Lady & seint Josep in þe forseyd
chirche of seint Thomas, & anoþer in þe worschepe of god &
oure lady & seint Johñ in þe chirche of· Haliwett, whiche schal
be holden & ruled in þe manere þat folweþ.

And first is ordeined þat alle þe bretheren & sostren of þis
fraternite schul vche Twelfday þe Midwynter be aff to-gedere at
þe masse in þe forseid chirche of seint Thomas, & heren
deuoutelich þilke masse, & offren þer-at in þe worschepe of god, of

97

gadere þat þat lakkeþ of þe bretheren, after þat hem nedeth, more or lasse.

Also is ordeined þat, if any brother go idel for defaute of werke & anoþer broþer haue werke wher-on he may werken his broþer, & þat werk be such þat his broþer conne wirche it, þan schal he werche his broþer to-fore any oþer þing, & ȝif hym als an other man wold take of hym for þe same wer[k].

Also is ordeined þat alle þe bretheren & sostren schul come to-gedere foure tymes aȝer be warnyng of þe maystres, at þe forseid chirche of seint Thomaȿ for to paie her quartrages, & to ordeine & byspeke þing þat is nedful & profitable for þe brotherede & helpyng of seke men.

Also is ordeined þat alle þo þat schul be receiued in to þis fraternite, þey schul be receiued by þe brotheren þat beþ at þilk assembles, by here aller assent, & non oþer tyme, & be charged to holden alle þese poyntes on amendement.

Also is ordeined þat no man ne woman be receyued in to þis fraternite bot onliche men & women of gode fame & of gode name.

Also is ordeined þat if any brother or soster, after þat he be receyued in to þis Fraternite, by-come of euel fame oþer of euel name, as thef, or comune barettour, or comune questmonger, or meyntenour of quereles, or be atteint of any falshede, þat anon he be put out of þe fraternite & neuermore come þer-jnne in no manere.

Also is ordeined þat what brother þat ne comeþ nouȝt atte somoñs of þe maistres atte forseid four tymes of þe ȝer, þat he paie a pound wex bot if he haue verrey excusacioñ of his abscense.

Also is ordeined þat vche ȝer þer schul four wardeines be chosen to reule þe fraternite þat ȝer, & to ordeine it & redresse it in þe beste manere.

Also is ordeined þat, if any debate be bytwené any of þe brotherede, þa[t] non of hem schal folwe aȝen oþer in none maner, til þe wardeines & þe bretheren han asayed wheþer þey ouꝛ lady & seint Josep, eche man a peny, and on midsomer day in þe forseid chirche of haliweꝥ at þe hye masse eche man a peny, & who so is absent at þilk masses wiþ-oute verry cause schal paie to þe brotherede a pound wex.

Also is ordeined þat vche brother & soster of þis fraternite schal paie to þe helpyng & susteynyng of seke men, whiche þat falle in dissese, as by falling doun of an hous, or hurtyng of an ax, or oþer diuerse sekenesses, twelfe penyes by þe ȝer.

Also is ordeined þat, whan any brother or soster of þis fraternite dyeþ wiþ-inne þe cite of london or in þe subarbes, þat alle þe bretheren & sostren schul hem gadere to-gedere at þe hous þer þe ded body is, & bring þe body to chirche, & ben at eue at þe Placebo & dirige & o morwe at þe masse, & offren, eche man a peny, & abide þer til þe cors be buried, & who so is absent at eue oþer on morwe withoute verrey cause paie a pound wex.

Also is ordeined þat, if any brother or soster dyeþ & haue nouȝt of his owen for to be buried, he schal be honestliche buried at þe costages of þe brothered.

Also is ordeined þat, if any brother or soster dieþ honeste deth out of London þe mountaunce of twelue myle & he haue nouȝt of wher-of to be buried of his owen, þan schul þe wardeynes of þe brotherede wenden þyder & burie hym on the comune costages of þe broþered.

Also is ordeined þat, if any broþer or soster falle in to pouert by goddes sonde, or in sekenes, or in any oþer dissese, as it is afore seyd, so þat he mowe not helpe hym self, þan schal he haue of þe brotherede vche woke fourtene penyes duryng his pouert, after he haþ lyne seke a fourten nyght. And þat he schal be so tymelich vesited & holpen þat he ne schal nouȝt, for defaute of help, be brouȝt to nouȝt, ne be vndon of his astat or he be holpe. And also he schal haue duryng his pouert clothyng as an other brother hath of þe brotherede on þe comune cost.

Also is ordeined þat, if þe comune box ne may nouȝt per-fourme þis fyndyng of suche seke breþeren, þan schul þey mowe accorden hem in gode manere, & if þey nulleth nouȝt accorden in þis maneŕ, vche do his beste by þe lawe, & þat no broþer meynte[yne e]yþer of hem preuelich ne apertliche in none manere.

Also is ordeined þat, what tyme þat any of þe bretheren or of þe sost[ren dyeþ, þey] schul haue a trental of messes out of þe comune box of þe forseid f[raternite], þat heŕ soules mowe þe better be holpen.

Also is ordeined þat vche soule mesday schal be seyde a t[rental of messes at þe] place þe bretheren wil assent for þe quike & for þe dede of þ[e fraternite & for all][5] cristen soules.

WORKS CITED

WORKS CITED

1. ASHLEY. "An Introduction to English Economic History and Theory." By W. J. Ashley. 2 vols. London: Longmans, Green & Co., 1906.
2. ATTON AND HOLLAND. "The King's Customs." By Henry Atton and Henry H. Holland. London: Murray, 1908.
3. AUBER. "China, an Outline of its Government, Laws and Policy." By Peter Auber. London: Parbury, Allen & Co., 1834.
4. "BRITISH RELATIONS with the Chinese Empire in 1832; Comparative Statement of the English and American Trade with India and Canton." Anon. London: Parbury, Allen & Co., 1832.
5. CRAWFURD. "The Chinese Monopoly Examined." By J. Crawfurd. London: Ames Ridgway, 1830.
6. DAVIS. "The Chinese." By John Francis Davis. London: Charles Knight & Co., 1836.
7. "DECENNIAL REPORTS of the Chinese Imperial Maritime Customs." First series, 1882–1891. Second series, 1892–1901; 2 vols.
8. EITEL. "Europe in China, the History of Hongkong." By E. J. Eitel. Hongkong: Kelly & Walsh, 1895.
9. "FACTS RELATING to Chinese Commerce in a Letter from a British Resident in China to his Friend in England." Anon. London: J. M. Richardson, 1829.
10. GUTZLAFF. "China Opened: or, a Display of the . . . Commerce . . . &c., of the Chinese Empire." By Charles Gutzlaff. 2 vols. London: Smith, Elder & Co., 1838.
11. HUNTER. "The Fan-Kwae at Canton before Treaty Days, 1825–1844." By an old Resident (W. C. Hunter). London: Kegan Paul, Trench & Co., 1882.
12. LJUNGSTEDT. "Contribution to an Historical Sketch of the Portuguese Settlements in China, &c." By A. L., Knt. (A. Ljungstedt). Macao: 1832.
13. MACGOWAN. "Chinese Guilds, or Chambers of Commerce and Trades Unions." By D. J. Macgowan, M.D. In Journal of North-China Branch of the Royal Asiatic Society, 1888–1889, pp. 133–192.
14. MARTIN. "China: Political, Commercial and Social." By R. Montgomery Martin. 2 vols. London: James Madden, 1847.

15. MATHESON. "The Present Position and Prospects of the British Trade with China." By James Matheson. London: Smith, Elder & Co., 1836.

16. NYE. "Peking the Goal: the Sole Hope of Peace." By Gideon Nye. Canton, 1873.

17. UNWIN. "The Gilds and Companies of London." By George Unwin. London: Methuen, 1908.

18. WILLIAMS. "The Middle Kingdom." By S. Wells Williams. New York: Scribners, 1907.

INDEX

INDEX

ABBREVIATIONS:

(Ch.) = Chinese, in China.
(Cn.) = Canton.

(Eng.) = English, in England.
(Ln.) = London.

ACCOUNTS, dates of settlement (Ch.), 42
Activity of gilds (Ch.), 3
Alien. *See* Foreign
Americans in China trade, 58, 83
Amoy, trade at, 58, 68
Apprentices (Eng.), 10, 19; (Ch.), 17, 30, 32
Arms, introduction prohibited (Cn.), 73
Association. *See* Fraternity
Audit of members' accounts (Ch.), 14, 15, 41

BAILIFF presiding over hallmoot (Eng.), 11
Barter, exchange of imports for exports, 52, 79
Benefits, personal, gilds claiming, 2, 49, 60, 67
Benevolent funds, administration of (Eng.), 7, 18, 31
Bequests to gild or fraternity (Eng.), 11, 13
Biting to death no murder (Ch.), 30
Bogue, entrance to river (Cn.), 64, 67, 72, 76
Boycott, application of, 5, 14, 21, 22, 23, 28, 30, 31, 48, 56, 57
Burgesses, action and authority (Eng.), 2, 19, 62

CANDLES and wax as fines, 17, 18, 28, 29, 87.
Canonised worthy, fraternity dedicated to (Ch.), 7, 38, 39
Canton, trade at, 58, 64, 67, 68, 81, 82
Cases taken before gild tribunal (Eng.), 25, 26; (Ch.), 27, 38, 43, 44, 56

Cemetery provided by gild (Ch.), 39, 47, 48
Cessation of business. *See* Boycott
Church, gild connexion with (Eng.), 16, 17. *See* Temple
Clannishness of Swatow men, 53
Clearing house, Bankers' gild as (Ch.), 12
Coercion of individual, 5, 27
Coffins for gild members (Ch.), 18, 40
Co-hong, action of (Cn.), 59, 70, 72, 80; formed (1720), 66; formally chartered (1760), 69; dissolved (1771), 69; re-established (1782), 70; abolished (1842), 84
Collective lordship (gild jurisdiction), 26
Combination of community, 27, 29, 53
Commission, rates of (Ch.), 15, 23, 51, 55
Committee of gild (Eng.), 12, 60; (Ch.), 12, 37, 49, 53
Commuting toll or tax by gild (Eng.), 11, 25; (Ch.), 27, 29
Comprador of ship (Cn.), 76, 77
Consoo guarantee fund (Cn.), 70, 80
Control of trade by gild (Eng.), 19, 60; (Ch.), 18, 40, 50, 53, 55, 67, 68, 75, 77, 78
Corvée duties of gild (Ch.), 12
Cotton, raw, value of (Cn.), 83
Country merchants (Cn.), 83
Court, weekly, of gild (Eng.), 11, 25, 26
Courts, national; cases removed from (Eng.), 25, 26, 27; (Ch.), 27, 38, 44, 56; trial of cases in (Eng.), 27; (Ch.), 27, 45

Craft gild, 9, 84
  (Eng.) Bakers (Ln.), 25
        Carpenters (Ln.), 86
        Drapers (Ln.), 10, 13, 17
        Fishmongers (Ln.), 25
        Goldsmiths (Ln.), 16
        Hatters (Ln.), 19
        Skinners (Ln.), 16
        Tailors (Ln.), 16
        Weavers (Ln.), 16, 25
        —— (Lincoln), 16
  (Ch.) Bankers (Ningpo), 10, 12, 15, 22
        —— (Shanghai), 21
        —— (Wuchow), 15
        —— (Wuhu), 14, 22
        Blacksmiths (Wenchow), 17
        Carpenters (Wenchow), 12
        Commission Agents (Wuchow), 15
        Druggists (Ningpo), 14
        —— (Wenchow), 10, 17, 23
        Fish-hook-makers (Wenchow), 11
        Fishmongers (Ningpo), 14, 23
        Goldbeaters (Soochow), 29
        —— (Wenchow), 11
        Millers (Wenchow), 12
        Needle-makers (Wenchow), 11
        Opium (Ningpo), 29
        —— (Wuchow), 15, 23
        Pawnbrokers (Wuchow), 15
        Servants (Shanghai), 31
        Silk (Shanghai), 21
        Silk-weavers (Wenchow), 17, 29, 33
        Stationers (Wuchow), 15
        Tea (Shanghai), 12, 14, 22
        —— (Hankow), 28
        Timber (Ningpo), 15
        (Wuchow), 15
        Wheelbarrow (Shanghai), 30
Credit, given or not given (Ch.), 24, 42

Dead, respect shown to (Eng.), 7, 18, 88; (Ch.), 18, 39, 47, 48

Debt, action in regard to (Eng.), 20; (Ch.), 23, 24
Debts due to foreign traders (Cn.), 69, 73; due by foreign traders (Cn.), 81
Delegation of powers to gild, 19, 20, 26, 27
Demi-god, fraternity or gild dedicated to (Ch.), 7, 17, 39, 55
Democratic organisation of gild (Ch.), 9, 12, 53
Deposit by gild member (Ch.), 14
Dinners; a gild function, 7, 17; as fine or on initiation (Ch.), 14, 28, 29, 42
Display of stocks required (Eng.), 19
Disputes settled by gild (Eng.), 25, 26, 90; (Ch.), 27, 29, 38, 43, 44, 55
Distrust of delegated authority (Ch.), 12
Dutch in China trade, 58, 82

East India Company, English (Cn.), 59, 69, 83, 84
Emperor. See Sovereign
Emperor's merchant (Cn.), 65
Endowment funds of gilds (Eng.), 13; (Ch.), 14
English in China trade, 58, 82, 83
Entrance fee in money (Ch.), 14, 15, 17, 41
Equality, national, assertion of (Cn.), 84
Ethical principles applied to business (Ch.), 21
Exclusion from gild (Ch.), 11
Extraterritoriality, instance of (Eng.), 63

Factories, foreign (Cn.), 57, 73, 74, 77, 80, 83
Farm. See Commuting
Fictitious. See Speculative
Fines, money, levied by gild (Ch.), 14, 28, 42, 51, 52, 55; other fines, see Candles, Dinners, Firecrackers, Theatrical
Fire risk on goods (Ch.), 42
Firecrackers as fines, 55
Foochow, trade at, 58
Foreign trader, relation to gild (Eng.), 10, 19, 20, 61, 62; (Ch.), 22, 28, 29, 56, 65, 67, 68, 70, 74, 75, 77, 80

Fortune, accumulation of, 4, 80, 81
Fraternity, religious, 7, 11, 13, 31
Fraternity precedent to craft gild (Eng.), 8, 16, 87
Free-traders, Americans as, 83
French authorities at Shanghai, action of, 46, 47
—— in China trade, 58, 82
Funerals. *See* Dead

GOVERNMENT, national, working of (Ch.), 1, 20. *See also* Officials
—— of gild (Eng.), 11, 60, 90; (Ch.), 12, 37, 49, 53
Governor, office of (Cn.), 72, 79

HALLMOOT of gild (Eng.), 11, 25, 26
Hanse. *See* Merchant gild
Hien, magistrate (Cn.), 72, 76, 79
Honourable character of merchants (Cn.), 80
Hoppo, action taken by (Cn.), 65, 67, 69, 71, 79, 80
Host, foreigner required to go to (Eng.), 62; (Ch.), 74
Hostility of alien merchants (Ch.), 37, 40, 44
Howqua, contributions and wealth (Cn.), 81
Hwei or Fraternity (Ch.), 7
Hwei-kwan, name of provincial club (Ch.), 35

IMPOSITIONS. *See* Taxes
Income of gild (Eng.), 13; (Ch.), 13, 38, 49, 54, 55
Independent initiative checked, 24
Inspection of wares, 19, 23
Interest, rate of (Ch.), 4, 69 *n.* 4, 73

JOURNEYMEN (Eng.), 20, 31, 89; (Ch.), 32, 34, 41
Judgment of gild decisive (Ch.), 15, 23
Jurisdiction over gild members (Eng.), 25, 60, 89; (Ch.), 27, 43

KING. *See* Sovereign
Kung-so; name of craft gild (Ch.), 9; occasional name of provincial club (Ch.), 35; Consoo fund (Cn.), 70

LAW, administration of (Eng.), 2, 27; (Ch.), 2, 4, 27, 80
Limit of foreigner's residence (Eng.), 62, 63; (Ch.), 74, 76
Loans from foreign traders (Eng.), 62, 64, 79
London had no gild merchant, 60
Loss on trade in English products (Cn.), 78

MACAO, place of foreign residence, 58, 74, 76
Manager of gild (Ch.), 37, 49, 50, 54. *See also* Warden
Markets, authority over (Eng.), 19; (Ch.), 51
Measurement charges on ships (Cn.), 66, 76
Measures, standard, 19, 23, 24, 43
Membership of gild (Eng.), 10, 60; (Ch.), 10, 36, 49; compulsory, 10, 36
Merchant gild (Eng.), 59, 61; Newchwang, 49; Swatow, 53; Canton, 57; not general (Ch.), 7
Mistery. *See* Craft gild
Money, transfer, at Newchwang, 52
Monopoly, English and Chinese compared, 79; of E. I. C., 83; abolished, 84
Monsoon and shipping, 75, 76
Mortuary provided by gild (Ch.), 40, 47, 48
Municipal government, 5, 9, 18, 20, 24, 26, 46, 49, 55

NAPIER, Lord, Chief Superintendent, 84
Newchwang Great Gild, 49
Ningpo, trade at, 58, 68
Number of apprentices, 30, 33

OFFICIALS, character of (Eng.), 1; (Ch.), 1, 21, 32, 35
—— protection against (Ch.), 1, 30, 36, 40, 44, 45, 54, 55, 56, 57
—— relation to gild (Ch.), 21, 37, 38, 39, 45, 64, 65, 70, 79, 81
Oligarchical government of gild (Eng.), 12; (Ch.), 37, 64
Opium, value of (Cn.), 83
Oppression. *See* Persecution
Origin of gilds (Eng.), 9, 87; (Ch.), 9, 36

Pageants, setting forth of, 18
Partnership between member and non-member (Ch.), 29, 42
People, character of (Eng.), 2; (Ch.), 1, 21
Persecution of offenders by gild, 5, 29, 55
Petitions, presentation of, by foreigners (Cn.), 74
Pleasure parties, restrictions on (Cn.), 73, 75
Political differences, East and West, 1
Portuguese in China trade, 58
Poverty of people (Ch.), 4
Prices and rates fixed by gild (Ch.), 12, 15, 21, 22, 23, 43, 50, 51, 78
—— inaccessible to foreigners (Cn.), 75, 78
Provincial club (Ch.), 35
    At Peking, 36, 37
    Canton, at Pakhoi, 44
    —— at Wuchow, 44
    Hanyang, at Ichang, 38, 41
    Hukwang, at Wuchow, 43
    Kiangnan, at Chungking, 38
    Ningpo, at Shanghai, 46
    —— at Wenchow, 40, 45
    Shantung, at Ningpo, 42
Public opinion, force of, 5, 21
Purchases by foreigners, restrictions on (Eng.), 62, 63; (Ch.), 74, 75, 78

Quality, maintenance of (Eng.), 19, 61
Quarterage from gild members (Eng.), 13, 87; (Ch.), 16

Rates. See Prices
Regulation of foreign trade (Eng.), 61; (Ch.), 64, 65, 72
Relations suspended pending unsettled dispute (Ch.), 22, 23
Religious feeling, intensity of (Eng.), 8, 16, 87.
Residents, foreign (Cn.), 82
Resistance to restrictions (Cn.), 63, 64, 67, 69.
Restrictions imposed on foreigners (Eng.), 19, 20, 62; (Ch.), 64, 65, 72
Revenues. See Income
Riot, instigated by gild (Ch.), 30, 31, 47, 48, avoided by gild, 55

Rotation in office (Ch.), 12, 15, 53
Rumour, effect of (Ch.), 5

Saint, fraternity dedicated to (Eng.), 7, 16, 17, 87
Sales by foreigners restricted (Eng.), 20, 62, 63; (Ch.), 74, 75, 77
Scales. See Measures
Secretary, permanent, of gild (Ch.), 13, 27, 37, 53, 54
Security merchant (Cn.), 68, 74, 75, 77, 78
Servants, Chinese, engagement by foreigners (Cn.), 65, 73, 77
Service as apprentice, 33
Settlements at Shanghai, status of, 46
Shiuhing, former viceregal seat (Cn.), 71
Sickness cared for (Eng.), 88
Social differences, East and West, 1
Sovereign, action of (Eng.), 1, 18, 62, 79; (Ch.), 64, 79
Spanish in China trade, 58
Speculative dealings prohibited (Ch.), 22, 43
Staple, Canton the, 57, 59, 68, 84
Steelyard, 7, 35, 57, 64
Storage of goods (Ch.), 42
Strike usually succeeds (Ch.), 32
Subscriptions from gild members (Eng.), 13, 87; (Ch.), 81
Supercargoes of E. I. C., action of (Cn.), 64, 65, 67
Swatow, characteristics of, 53

Tang, occasional name of craft gild (Ch.), 9
Tax levied by gild (Ch.), 14, 15, 41
Taxes imposed on foreigners (Cn.), 66, 67, 69, 76, 77
Temple, gild connexion with (Ch.), 17, 32, 39. See Church
Theatrical performance (Ch.), a gild function, 16, 39; as fine, 28, 29, 42
Toll. See Tax
Trade at Canton, value, 82
—— operations of, 3
—— unions, 32
Tronage, right of (Eng.), 19
Transfer money, 52

Unemployment of gild members (Eng.), 89

VICEROY, action of (Cn.), 67, 69, 71, 79

WALKING, sole mode of progression (Cn.), 73

Warships, restrictions on (Cn.), 72

Wardens of gilds (Eng.), 10, 11, 19, 32, 60, 88. See Manager Ch.)

Wax. See Candles

Women, introduction prohibited (Cn.), 73

——Members of gilds (Eng.), 88

Workmen. See Journeymen

Worship, common, of gilds (Eng.), 16, 87; (Ch.), 17, 39